Chocolate

Parragon

Bath New York Singapore Hong Kong Cologne Delhi Melbourne

This edition published by Parragon in 2009

Parragon Publishing
Queen Street House
4 Queen Street
Bath BA1 1HE, UK

ISBN 978-1-4075-8027-2

Printed in China

Notes for the Reader
This book uses imperial, metric, and U.S. cup measurements. Follow the same units of measurement throughout; do not mix imperial and metric. All spoon measurements are level: teaspoons are assumed to be 5 ml, and tablespoons are assumed to be 15 ml. Unless otherwise stated, milk is assumed to be whole, eggs and individual vegetables, such as potatoes, are medium, and pepper is freshly ground black pepper.

The times given are an approximate guide only. Preparation times differ according to the techniques used by different people and the cooking times may also vary from those given as a result of the type of oven used. Optional ingredients, variations, or serving suggestions have not been included in the calculations.

Recipes using raw or very lightly cooked eggs should be avoided by infants, the elderly, pregnant women, convalescents, and anyone with a chronic condition. Pregnant and breastfeeding women are advised to avoid eating peanuts and peanut products. People with nut allergies should be aware that some of the prepared ingredients used in the recipes in this book may contain nuts. Always check the packaging before use.

Picture acknowledgements
The publisher would like to thank gulfimages/Getty Images for permission to reproduce copyright material for the front cover

Chocolate

introduction

The very word "chocolate" almost has a magic about it and those who love it will agree unanimously that the taste is quite definitely magical.

The remarkable story of chocolate dates back to the 7th century, when the cocoa tree, *Theobroma cacao*, was cultivated by the Maya of Central America. This ancient civilization established a flourishing trade, even using the cocoa bean as currency. The explorer Christopher Columbus took the cocoa bean to Spain in 1502, and Hernán Cortés, who conquered Mexico for Spain, soon afterward got an idea of what to do with this curious object when the Aztec Emperor Montezuma introduced him

to *xocotlatl*, a drink made of crushed, roasted cocoa beans and cold water. This bitter-tasting brew soon evolved into something more pleasant when it was served hot with a flavoring of vanilla, spices, honey, and sugar.

By the late 17th century, Europe and beyond had fallen under the spell of the "hot chocolate" drink, but it is a 19th-century Dutch chemist, Coenraad Van Houten, whom we have to thank for chocolate that we can eat. This veritable hero invented a method of producing pure cocoa butter and a hard "cake" that could be milled to produce cocoa "powder" for flavoring. Within a very short time, the chocolate industry was founded, going from strength to strength as different countries began to produce smooth, melt-in-the-mouth chocolate bars.

Today—to our delight—there is no end to the creative ways in which chocolate is used in cooking. Hot desserts, cakes, cookies, chilled desserts, ice creams—they all seem to have a little extra

appeal when they include chocolate. Even the original concept, hot chocolate, has been miraculously transformed into an exceptionally good cheesecake.

If you are one of the world's many chocoholics, you'll love this book. Just dip in and be indulgent!

favorite desserts

In this chapter you'll find a few of the favorite traditional chocolate dessert recipes. You'll also find several traditional recipes given a modern twist by transforming them with chocolate! For example, you might have tried a classic lemon meringue pie, but have you thought of trying a rich, creamy chocolate filling beneath that melting meringue topping? Adding a touch of cocoa to make a pecan pie or bread pudding even more delectable? Or finishing off a special dinner party with a superb flourish—a stylish Italian zabaglione, but with chocolate?

Chocolate marries very successfully with fruit, as you'll soon discover. Fold your favorite fruits inside a chocolate crêpe, add a handful of chocolate chips to a fruit crumble topping, or dunk chilled fruit into a warm chocolate fondue. Make the most of the brief season for blueberries and blackberries with flans, pies, and possibly the most delicious chocolate steamed pudding you'll ever taste, served with a rum syrup.

An important tip to bear in mind when making any recipe that includes chocolate is to use a top-quality product with the highest cocoa butter content you can find—around 70 percent—as this gives a far superior taste. It might cost a little more but you will get a really excellent result.

fine chocolate tart

ingredients

SERVES 6

pie dough

5 oz/150 g/generous ¾ cup
    all-purpose flour
2 tsp unsweetened cocoa
2 tsp confectioners' sugar
pinch of salt
1¾ oz/50 g cold butter,
    cut into pieces
1 egg yolk
ice-cold water

ganache filling

7 oz/200 g semisweet
    chocolate with
    70% cocoa solids
2 tbsp unsalted butter,
    softened
9 fl oz/250 ml/1 cup
    heavy cream
1 tsp dark rum (optional)
chocolate curls, to serve

method

1 Lightly grease a 9-inch/22-cm loose-bottom fluted tart pan. Sift the flour, cocoa, confectioners' sugar, and salt into a food processor, add the butter, and process until the mixture resembles fine bread crumbs. Tip the mixture into a large bowl, add the egg yolk, and add a little ice-cold water, just enough to bring the dough together. Turn out onto a counter dusted with more flour and cocoa and roll out the dough 3¼ inches/ 8 cm larger than the pan. Carefully lift the dough into the pan and press to fit. Roll the rolling pin over the pan to neaten the edges and trim the excess dough. Fit a piece of parchment paper into the tart shell, fill with dried beans, and let chill in the refrigerator for 30 minutes.

2 Remove the pastry shell from the refrigerator and bake in a preheated oven, 375°F/190°C, for 15 minutes, then remove the beans and paper and bake for an additional 5 minutes.

3 To make the ganache filling, chop the chocolate and put in a bowl with the softened butter. Bring the cream to a boil, then pour onto the chocolate, stirring well, add the rum (if using) and continue stirring to make sure the chocolate is melted completely. Pour into the pastry shell and let chill for 3 hours. Serve decorated with chocolate curls.

white chocolate & cardamom tart

ingredients

SERVES 6

pie dough

5 oz/150 g/generous $^3/4$ cup
    all-purpose flour
pinch of salt
$2^1/2$ oz/75 g cold butter,
    cut into pieces
cold water

filling

seeds of 8 cardamom pods
12 oz/350 g white chocolate,
    chopped into small pieces
2 pieces or $^1/4$ oz/6 g fine
    leaf gelatin
cold water
15 fl oz/425 ml/generous
    $1^1/2$ cups whipping cream

shavings of white chocolate,
    to decorate

method

1 Sift the flour and salt into a food processor, add the butter, and process until the mixture resembles fine bread crumbs. Tip into a large bowl and add just enough cold water to bring the dough together. Turn out onto a lightly floured counter and roll out the dough 3$^1/4$ inches/8 cm larger than the pan. Carefully lift the dough into a lightly greased 9-inch/22-cm loose-bottom fluted tart pan and press to fit. Roll the rolling pin over the pan to trim the excess dough. Fit a piece of parchment paper into the tart shell and fill with dried beans.

2 Let chill for 30 minutes, then remove from the refrigerator and bake blind for 15 minutes in a preheated oven, 375°F/190°C. Remove the beans and paper and bake for an additional 10 minutes. Let cool completely.

3 Crush the cardamom seeds until powdery and put in a large bowl with the chocolate. Soak the gelatin in a little cold water in a small heat-proof bowl for 5 minutes, then stir over a pan of simmering water until dissolved. At the same time, in a separate pan, heat the cream until just boiling, then pour over the chocolate, using a whisk to stir until the chocolate has melted. Add the gelatin and stir the mixture until smooth. Let cool and pour into the tart shell, then let chill for at least 3 hours.

chocolate fudge tart

ingredients

SERVES 6–8

flour, for sprinkling

12 oz/350 g ready-made
  unsweetened pie dough

confectioners' sugar, for
  dusting

filling

5 oz/140 g semisweet
  chocolate, finely chopped

6 oz/175 g butter, diced

12 oz/350 g/1³/4 cups golden
  granulated sugar

3¹/2 oz/100 g/³/4 cup
  all-purpose flour

¹/2 tsp vanilla extract

6 eggs, beaten

to decorate

5 fl oz/150 ml/
  ²/3 cup whipped cream

ground cinnamon

method

1 Roll out the pie dough on a lightly floured counter and use to line an 8-inch/20-cm deep loose-bottom tart pan. Prick the dough base lightly with a fork, then line with foil and fill with pie weights. Bake in a preheated oven, 400°F/200°C, for 12–15 minutes, or until the dough no longer looks raw. Remove the beans and foil and bake for an additional 10 minutes, or until the dough is firm. Let cool. Reduce the oven temperature to 350°F/180°C.

2 To make the filling, place the chocolate and butter in a heatproof bowl and set over a pan of gently simmering water until melted. Stir until smooth, then remove from the heat and let cool. Place the sugar, flour, vanilla extract, and eggs in a separate bowl and whisk until well blended. Stir in the butter and chocolate mixture.

3 Pour the filling into the pastry shell and bake in the oven for 50 minutes, or until the filling is just set. Transfer to a wire rack to cool completely. Dust with confectioners' sugar before serving with whipped cream sprinkled lightly with cinnamon.

lemon & chocolate tart

ingredients

SERVES 8–10

3$^1/_2$ oz/100 g/$^3/_4$ cup
    all-purpose flour
1 oz/25 g/$^1/_4$ cup
    unsweetened cocoa
2$^3/_4$ oz/75 g butter
1 oz/25 g/$^1/_4$ cup ground
    almonds
1$^3/_4$ oz/50 g/$^1/_4$ cup golden
    superfine sugar
1 egg, beaten
chocolate curls, to decorate

filling

4 eggs
1 egg yolk
7 oz/200 g/1 cup golden
    superfine sugar
5 fl oz/150 ml/$^2/_3$ cup
    heavy cream
grated rind and juice of
    2 lemons

method

1 Sift the flour and unsweetened cocoa into a food processor. Add the butter, almonds, sugar, and egg and process until the mixture forms a ball. Gather the dough together and press into a flattened ball. Place in the center of an 8$^1/_2$-inch/22-cm loose-bottom tart pan and press evenly over the bottom of the pan with your fingers, then work the pie dough up the sides with your thumbs. Allow any excess dough to go over the edge. Cover and let chill for 30 minutes.

2 Roll the rolling pin over the pan to trim the excess dough. Prick the dough base lightly with a fork, then line with parchment paper and fill with pie weights. Bake in a preheated oven, 400°F/200°C, for 12–15 minutes, or until the dough no longer looks raw. Remove the weights and paper, return to the oven and bake for 10 minutes, or until the pastry is firm. Let cool. Reduce the oven temperature to 300°F/150°C.

3 To make the filling, whisk the whole eggs, egg yolk, and sugar together until smooth. Add the cream and whisk again, then stir in the lemon rind and juice. Pour the filling into the pastry shell and bake for 50 minutes, or until just set. When the tart is cooked, remove the tart ring and let cool. Decorate with chocolate curls before serving.

blackberry chocolate flan

ingredients

SERVES 6

pie dough

6 oz/175 g/1 cup all-purpose
   flour, plus extra for dusting
1 oz/30 g/generous ¼ cup
   unsweetened cocoa
2 oz/55 g/½ cup
   confectioners' sugar
pinch of salt
3 oz/85 g unsalted butter,
   cut into small pieces
½ egg yolk

filling

10 fl oz/300 ml/1¼ cups
   heavy cream
6 oz/175 g blackberry jelly
8 oz/225 g semisweet
   chocolate, broken into
   pieces
2 tbsp unsalted butter,
   cut into small pieces

sauce

1 lb 8 oz/675 g blackberries,
   plus extra for decoration
1 tbsp lemon juice
2 tbsp superfine sugar
2 tbsp crème de cassis

method

1 To make the pie dough, sift the flour, cocoa, confectioners' sugar, and salt into a mixing bowl and make a well in the center. Place the butter and egg yolk in the well and gradually mix in the dry ingredients using a pastry blender. Knead lightly and form into a ball. Wrap the dough and let chill in the refrigerator for 1 hour.

2 Roll out the dough on a lightly floured counter and use to line a 12 x 4-inch/ 30 x 10-cm rectangular tart pan. Prick the base with a fork, line with parchment paper, and fill with dried beans. Bake in a preheated oven, 350°F/180°C, for 15 minutes. Remove from the oven, and set aside to cool.

3 To make the filling, place the cream and jelly in a pan and bring to a boil over low heat. Remove from the heat and stir in the chocolate and then the butter until melted and smooth. Pour the mixture into the pastry shell and set aside to cool.

4 To make the sauce, whiz the blackberries, lemon juice, and superfine sugar in a food processor until smooth. Strain through a nylon sieve into a bowl and stir in the cassis.

5 Transfer the flan to a serving plate. Arrange the remaining blackberries on top and brush with a little blackberry and liqueur sauce. Serve with the remaining sauce on the side.

boston crème pie

ingredients

SERVES 6

8 oz/225 g ready-prepared
   pie dough

filling

3 eggs

4 oz/115 g/scant $^2/_3$ cup
   superfine sugar

5 oz/150 g/generous $^3/_8$ cup
   all-purpose flour, plus
   extra for dusting

1 tbsp confectioners' sugar

pinch of salt

1 tsp vanilla extract

14 fl oz/400 ml/1$^3/_4$ cups milk

5 fl oz/150 ml/$^2/_3$ cup
   plain yogurt

5$^1/_2$ oz/150 g semisweet
   chocolate, broken into
   pieces

2 tbsp Kirsch

to decorate

5 fl oz/150 ml/$^2/_3$ cup
   sour cream

8 oz/225 g semisweet
   chocolate shavings
   or caraque

method

1 Roll out the pie dough and use to line a 9-inch/23-cm loose-bottom tart pan. Prick the base with a fork, line with parchment paper, and fill with dried beans. Bake in a preheated oven, 400°F/200°C, for 20 minutes. Remove the beans and paper and return the pastry shell to the oven for an additional 5 minutes. Remove from the oven and place on a wire rack to cool.

2 To make the filling, beat the eggs and superfine sugar in a heatproof bowl until fluffy. Sift in the flour, confectioners' sugar, and salt. Stir in the vanilla extract.

3 Bring the milk and yogurt to a boil in a small pan and strain it over the egg mixture. Set the bowl over a pan of barely simmering water. Stir the custard until it coats the back of a spoon.

4 Gently heat the chocolate with the Kirsch in a separate small pan until the chocolate has melted. Stir into the custard. Remove from the heat and stand the bowl in cold water. Let cool.

5 Pour the chocolate mixture into the pastry shell. Spread the sour cream evenly over the chocolate and decorate with chocolate shavings or caraque.

chocolate meringue pie

ingredients

SERVES 6

8 oz/225 g semisweet
   chocolate graham
   crackers
4 tbsp butter

filling

3 egg yolks
4 tbsp superfine sugar
4 tbsp cornstarch
1 pint/600 ml/2^1/$_2$ cups milk
3^1/$_2$ oz/100 g semisweet
   chocolate, melted

meringue

2 egg whites
3^1/$_2$ oz/100 g/^{1}/$_2$ cup
   superfine sugar
^{1}/$_4$ tsp vanilla extract

method

1 Place the crackers in a plastic bag and crush with a rolling pin, then transfer to a large bowl. Place the butter in a small, heavy-bottom pan and heat gently until just melted, then stir it into the cracker crumbs until well mixed. Press into the bottom and up the sides of a 9-inch/23-cm tart pan or dish.

2 To make the filling, place the egg yolks, superfine sugar, and cornstarch in a large bowl and beat until they form a smooth paste, adding a little of the milk, if necessary. Place the milk into a small, heavy-bottom pan and heat gently until almost boiling, then slowly pour it onto the egg mixture, whisking well.

3 Return the mixture to the pan and cook gently, whisking, until thick. Remove from the heat. Whisk in the melted chocolate, then pour it onto the cracker base.

4 To make the meringue, whisk the egg whites in a large, spotlessly clean, greasefree bowl until soft peaks form. Gradually whisk in two-thirds of the sugar until the mixture is stiff and glossy. Fold in the remaining sugar and vanilla extract.

5 Spread the meringue over the filling, swirling the surface with the back of a spoon to give it an attractive finish. Bake in the center of a preheated oven, 375°F/160°C, for 30 minutes, or until golden. Serve hot or just warm.

chocolate chiffon pie

ingredients

SERVES 8

nut base

8 oz/225 g/scant 2 cups
   shelled Brazil nuts

4 tbsp granulated sugar

4 tsp melted butter

filling

8 fl oz/225 ml/1 cup milk

2 tsp powdered gelatin

4 oz/115 g/generous $\frac{1}{2}$ cup
   superfine sugar

2 eggs, separated

8 oz/225 g semisweet
   chocolate, roughly
   chopped

1 tsp vanilla extract

5 fl oz/150 ml/^{2}/$_3$ cup
   heavy cream

2 tbsp chopped Brazil nuts,
   to decorate

method

1 Process the whole Brazil nuts in a food processor until finely ground. Add the granulated sugar and melted butter and process briefly to combine. Tip the mixture into a 9-inch/23-cm round tart pan and press it onto the base and side with a spoon. Bake in a preheated oven, 400°F/200°C, for 8–10 minutes, or until light golden brown. Set aside to cool.

2 Pour the milk into a heatproof bowl and sprinkle the gelatin over the surface. Let it soften for 2 minutes, then set over a pan of gently simmering water. Stir in half of the superfine sugar, both the egg yolks, and all the chocolate. Stir constantly over low heat for 4–5 minutes until the gelatin has dissolved and the chocolate has melted. Remove from the heat and beat until smooth. Stir in the vanilla extract, wrap and let chill in the refrigerator for 45–60 minutes until starting to set.

3 Whip the cream until it is stiff, then fold all but 3 tablespoons into the chocolate mixture. Whisk the egg whites in a separate, clean, greasefree bowl until soft peaks form. Add 2 teaspoons of the remaining sugar and whisk until stiff peaks form. Fold in the remaining sugar, then fold the egg whites into the chocolate mixture. Pour the filling into the pastry shell and let chill in the refrigerator for 3 hours. Decorate the pie with the remaining whipped cream and the chopped nuts before serving.

pecan & chocolate pie

ingredients

SERVES 6–8

pie dough

6 oz/175 g/scant $^1/_2$ cup
   all-purpose flour, plus
   extra for dusting
3$^1/_2$ oz /100 g butter, diced
1 tbsp golden superfine sugar
1 egg yolk, beaten with
   1 tbsp water

filling

2 oz/55 g butter
3 tbsp unsweetened cocoa
8 fl oz/225 ml/1 cup
   corn syrup
3 eggs
2$^1/_2$ oz/70 g/$^3/_8$ cup firmly
   packed dark brown sugar
6 oz/175 g/$^3/_4$ cup shelled
   pecans, chopped

to serve

whipped cream
ground cinnamon,
   for dusting

method

1 To make the pie dough, sift the flour into a large bowl. Rub in the butter until the mixture resembles fine bread crumbs, then stir in the superfine sugar. Stir in the beaten egg yolk. Knead lightly to form a firm dough, cover with plastic wrap, and let chill in the refrigerator for 1$^1/_2$ hours. Roll out the chilled dough on a lightly floured counter and use it to line an 8-inch/20-cm tart pan.

2 To make the filling, place the butter in a small, heavy-bottom pan and heat gently until melted. Sift in the cocoa and stir in the syrup. Place the eggs and sugar in a large bowl and beat together. Add the syrup mixture and the chopped pecans and stir. Pour the mixture into the prepared pastry shell.

3 Place the pie on a preheated cookie sheet and bake in a preheated oven, 375°F/190°C, for 35–40 minutes, or until the filling is just set. Let cool slightly and serve warm with a spoonful of whipped cream, dusted with ground cinnamon.

mississippi mud pie

ingredients

SERVES 8

pie dough

8 oz/225 g/scant 1⁵/₈ cups
   all-purpose flour, plus
   extra for dusting
2 tbsp unsweetened cocoa
5¹/₂ oz/150 g butter
2 tbsp superfine sugar
1–2 tbsp cold water

filling

6 oz/175 g butter
12 oz/350 g/scant 1³/₄ cups
   packed brown sugar
4 eggs, lightly beaten
4 tbsp unsweetened cocoa,
   sifted
5¹/₂ oz/150 g semisweet
   chocolate
10 fl oz/300 ml/1¹/₄ cups
   light cream
1 tsp chocolate extract

to decorate

15 fl oz/425 ml/scant 2 cups
   heavy cream, whipped
chocolate flakes and curls

method

1 To make the pie dough, sift the flour and cocoa into a mixing bowl. Rub in the butter with the fingertips until the mixture resembles fine bread crumbs. Stir in the sugar and enough cold water to mix to a soft dough. Wrap the dough and let chill in the refrigerator for 15 minutes.

2 Roll out the dough on a lightly floured counter and use to line a 9-inch/23-cm loose-bottom tart pan or ceramic pie dish. Line with parchment paper and fill with dried beans. Bake in a preheated oven, 375°F/190°C, for 15 minutes. Remove from the oven and take out the paper and beans. Bake the pastry shell for an additional 10 minutes.

3 To make the filling, beat the butter and sugar together in a bowl and gradually beat in the eggs with the cocoa. Melt the chocolate and beat it into the mixture with the light cream and the chocolate extract.

4 Reduce the oven temperature to 325°F/160°C. Pour the mixture into the pastry shell and bake for 45 minutes, or until the filling has set gently.

5 Let the mud pie cool completely, then transfer it to a serving plate, if you like. Cover with the whipped cream. Decorate the pie with chocolate flakes and curls and then let chill until ready to serve.

chocolate crumble pie

ingredients

SERVES 8

pie dough

7 oz/200 g/scant 1¹/4 cups
   all-purpose flour
1 tsp baking powder
4 oz/115 g unsalted butter,
   cut into small pieces
1 oz/25 g/generous ¹/4 cup
   superfine sugar
1 egg yolk
1–2 tsp cold water

filling

5 fl oz/150 ml/²/3 cup
   heavy cream
5 fl oz/150 ml/²/3 cup milk
8 oz/225 g semisweet
   chocolate, chopped
2 eggs

crumble topping

3¹/2 oz/100 g/generous
   ¹/2 cup packed
   brown sugar
3 oz/85 g/³/4 cup
   toasted pecans
4 oz/115 g semisweet
   chocolate
3 oz/85 g amaretti cookies
1 tsp unsweetened cocoa

method

1 To make the pie dough, sift the flour and baking powder into a large bowl, rub in the butter, and stir in the sugar, then add the egg and a little water to bring the dough together. Turn the dough out, and knead briefly. Wrap the dough and let chill in the refrigerator for 30 minutes.

2 Preheat the oven to 375°F/190°C. Roll out the pie dough and use to line a 9-inch/23-cm loose-bottom tart pan. Prick the pastry shell with a fork. Line with parchment paper and fill with dried beans. Bake in the oven for 15 minutes. Remove from the oven and take out the paper and beans. Reduce the oven temperature to 350°F/180°C.

3 Bring the cream and milk to a boil in a pan, remove from the heat, and add the chocolate. Stir until melted and smooth. Beat the eggs and add to the chocolate mixture, mix thoroughly and pour into the shell. Bake for 15 minutes, remove from the oven, and let rest for 1 hour.

4 When you are ready to serve the pie, place the topping ingredients in the food processor and pulse to chop. (If you do not have a processor, place the sugar in a large bowl, chop the nuts and chocolate with a large knife, and crush the cookies, then add to the bowl with the cocoa and mix well.) Sprinkle over the pie, then serve it in slices.

chocolate blueberry pies

ingredients

MAKES 10

pie dough

7 oz/200 g/scant 1¹/4 cups
     all-purpose flour
2oz/55 g/¹/2 cup
     unsweetened cocoa
2oz/55 g/generous ¹/4 cup
     superfine sugar
pinch of salt
4¹/2 oz/125 g butter, cut
     into small pieces
1 egg yolk
1–2 tbsp cold water

sauce

6 oz/200 g/1³/8 cups
     blueberries
2 tbsp crème de cassis
¹/2 oz/10 g/scant ¹/8 cup
     confectioners' sugar, sifted

filling

5 oz/140 g semisweet
     chocolate
1 cup heavy cream
5fl oz/150 ml/²/3 cup
     sour cream

method

1 To make the pie dough, place the flour, cocoa, sugar, and salt in a large bowl and rub in the butter until the mixture resembles bread crumbs. Add the egg and a little cold water to form a dough. Wrap the dough and let chill in the refrigerator for 30 minutes.

2 Remove the pie dough from the refrigerator and roll out. Use to line 10 x 4-inch/10-cm tart pans. Freeze for 30 minutes. Preheat the oven to 350°F/180°C. Bake the pastry shells in the oven for 15–20 minutes. Let cool.

3 To make the sauce, place the blueberries, cassis, and the confectioners' sugar in a pan and warm through so that the berries become shiny but do not burst. Let cool.

4 To make the filling, melt the chocolate in a heatproof bowl set over a pan of simmering water, then let cool slightly. Whip the cream until stiff and fold in the sour cream and chocolate.

5 Remove the pastry shells to a serving plate and divide the chocolate filling between them, smoothing the surface with a spatula, then top with the blueberries.

hot chocolate cheesecake

ingredients

SERVES 8

butter, for greasing

pie dough

5^1/$_2$ oz/150 g/generous 1 cup
all-purpose flour

2 tbsp unsweetened cocoa

2^3/$_4$ oz/75 g butter, diced

2 tbsp golden superfine sugar

1 oz/25 g/^{1}/$_4$ cup ground
almonds

1 egg yolk

filling

2 eggs, separated

2^3/$_4$ oz/75 g/scant ^{3}/$_8$ cup
golden superfine sugar

12 oz/350 g/1^1/$_2$ cups
cream cheese

1^1/$_2$ oz/40 g/^{3}/$_8$ cup
ground almonds

5fl oz/150 ml/^{2}/$_3$ cup
heavy cream

1 oz/25 g/^{1}/$_4$ cup
unsweetened
cocoa, sifted

1 tsp vanilla extract

confectioners' sugar,
for dusting

method

1 To make the pie dough, sift the flour and unsweetened cocoa into a bowl. Add the butter and rub it in until the mixture resembles fine bread crumbs. Stir in the sugar and almonds. Add the egg yolk and enough water to make a soft dough. Roll out on a lightly floured counter and use to line an 8-inch/20-cm loose-bottom cake pan greased with butter. Let chill in the refrigerator while preparing the filling.

2 To make the filling, place the egg yolks and superfine sugar in a large bowl and whisk together until thick and pale. Whisk in the cheese, almonds, cream, cocoa, and vanilla extract until blended.

3 Place the egg whites in a clean, greasefree bowl and whisk until stiff but not dry. Stir a little of the whisked egg whites into the cheese mixture, then fold in the remainder. Pour into the pastry shell. Bake in a preheated oven, 325°F/160°C, for 1^1/$_2$ hours, or until risen and just firm to the touch. Remove from the pan and dust with confectioners' sugar.

chocolate bread pudding

ingredients

SERVES 4

6 thick slices white bread,
   crusts removed

16 fl oz/450 ml/scant
   2 cups milk

6 fl oz/175 ml canned
   evaporated milk

2 tbsp unsweetened cocoa

2 eggs

2 tbsp brown sugar

1 tsp vanilla extract

confectioners' sugar,
   for dusting

hot fudge sauce

2 oz/55 g semisweet
   chocolate, broken
   into pieces

1 tbsp unsweetened cocoa

2 tbsp light corn syrup

2 oz/55 g/$^1/_4$ cup butter or
   margarine

2 tbsp brown sugar

5 fl oz/150 ml/$^2/_3$ cup milk

1 tbsp cornstarch

method

1 Grease a shallow ovenproof dish. Cut the bread into squares and layer them in the dish.

2 Put the milk, evaporated milk, and the unsweetened cocoa in a pan and heat gently, stirring occasionally, until the mixture is lukewarm. Whisk the eggs, sugar, and vanilla extract together. Add the warm milk mixture and beat well.

3 Pour into the prepared dish, making sure that all the bread is completely covered. Cover the dish with plastic wrap and let chill in the refrigerator for 1–2 hours, then bake in a preheated oven 350°F/180°C, for 35–40 minutes, until set. Let stand for 5 minutes.

4 To make the sauce, put all the ingredients into a pan and heat gently, stirring constantly until smooth.

5 Dust the chocolate bread pudding with confectioners' sugar and serve immediately with the hot fudge sauce.

saucy chocolate pudding

ingredients

SERVES 4–6

3 oz/85 g butter, softened,
plus extra for greasing
2 oz/55 g/scant $^{1}/_{2}$ cup
self-rising flour
1 oz/25 g/$^{1}/_{4}$ cup
unsweetened cocoa
1 tsp ground cinnamon
4 oz/115 g/generous $^{1}/_{2}$ cup
golden superfine sugar
1 egg
2 tbsp dark brown sugar
2 oz/55 g/$^{1}/_{4}$ cup shelled
pecans, chopped
10 fl oz/300 ml/1$^{1}/_{4}$ cups
hot black coffee
confectioners' sugar,
for dusting
whipped cream, to serve

method

1 Grease a shallow 2$^{3}/_{4}$-pint/1.2-liter/5-cup ovenproof dish with a little butter. Sift the flour, unsweetened cocoa, and cinnamon into a large bowl. Add the butter, 3 oz/85 g/$^{3}/_{8}$ cup of the superfine sugar, and the egg and beat together until the mixture is well blended. Turn into the prepared dish and sprinkle with the dark brown sugar and the pecans.

2 Pour the coffee into a large pitcher, stir in the remaining superfine sugar until dissolved and carefully pour over the pudding.

3 Bake in a preheated oven, 325°F/160°C, for 50–60 minutes, or until firm to the touch in the center. Dust with a little confectioners' sugar and serve with whipped cream.

chocolate fruit crumble

ingredients

SERVES 4

6 tbsp butter, plus extra
   for greasing

14 oz/400 g canned apricots,
   in natural juice

1 lb/450 g cooking apples,
   peeled and thickly sliced

3^1/$_2$ oz/100 g/scant ^{2}/$_3$ cup
   all-purpose flour

1^3/$_4$ oz/50 g/^{1}/$_2$ cup rolled
   oats

4 tbsp superfine sugar

3^1/$_2$ oz/100 g/generous
   ^{1}/$_2$ cup chocolate chips

method

1 Drain the apricots, reserving 4 tablespoons of the juice. Place the apples and apricots in a greased ovenproof dish with the reserved apricot juice and toss to mix thoroughly.

2 Sift the flour into a large bowl. Cut the butter into small cubes and rub it in with your fingertips until the mixture resembles fine bread crumbs. Stir in the rolled oats, superfine sugar, and chocolate chips.

3 Sprinkle the crumble mixture over the apples and apricots and level the top roughly. Do not press the crumble down onto the fruit. Bake in a preheated oven, 180°C/350°F, for 40–45 minutes, or until the topping is golden. Serve the crumble hot or cold.

blueberry chocolate pudding with rum syrup

ingredients

SERVES 4

4 oz/115 g butter, softened,
    plus extra for greasing

4 oz/115 g/²/₃ cup soft
    brown sugar

2 eggs

5¹/₂ oz/150 g/²/₃ cup
    all-purpose flour

¹/₂ tsp baking powder

2 tbsp unsweetened cocoa
    powder

4 oz/114 g/³/₄ cup blueberries

rum syrup

4 oz/120 g dark chocolate,
    chopped

2 tbsp maple syrup

1 tbsp unsalted butter

1 tbsp rum

whole blueberries, to decorate

method

1 Grease a large pudding basin. Heat water to a depth of 3–4 inches/7.5–10 cm in a large pan over low heat until simmering.

2 Put the butter, sugar, eggs, flour, baking powder, and cocoa powder into a large bowl and beat together until thoroughly mixed. Stir in the blueberries. Spoon the mixture into the prepared basin and cover tightly with two layers of foil. Carefully place the basin in the pan of simmering water, ensuring that the water level is comfortably lower than the basin's rim. Steam the pudding for 1 hour, topping up the water when necessary.

3 About 5 minutes before the end of the cooking time, heat the ingredients for the rum syrup in a small pan over low heat, stirring, until smooth and melted. Remove the pudding from the heat, discard the foil, and run a knife around the edge to loosen the pudding. Turn out onto a serving dish, pour over the syrup, and decorate with blueberries. Serve immediately.

exotic fruit chocolate crêpes

ingredients

SERVES 4

3¹/₂ oz/100 g/³/₄ cup
   all-purpose flour
2 tbsp unsweetened cocoa
pinch of salt
1 egg, beaten
10 fl oz/300 ml/1¹/₄ cups milk
oil, for frying
confectioners' sugar,
   for dusting

filling

3¹/₂ oz/100 g/scant ¹/₂ cup
   strained plain yogurt
9 oz/250 g/1¹/₈ cups
   mascarpone cheese
confectioners' sugar (optional)
1 mango, peeled and diced
8 oz/225 g/generous 1 cup
   strawberries, hulled
   and quartered
2 passion fruit

method

1 To make the filling, place the yogurt and mascarpone cheese in a bowl and sweeten with confectioners' sugar, if you like. Place the mango and strawberries in a bowl and mix together. Cut the passion fruit in half, scoop out the pulp and seeds, and add to the mango and strawberries. Stir together, then set aside.

2 To make the crêpes, sift the flour, unsweetened cocoa, and salt into a bowl and make a well in the center. Add the egg and whisk with a balloon whisk. Gradually beat in the milk, drawing in the flour from the sides, to make a smooth batter. Cover and let stand for 20 minutes. Heat a small amount of oil in a 7-inch/18-cm crêpe pan or skillet. Pour in just enough batter to thinly coat the bottom of the pan. Cook over medium–high heat for 1 minute, then turn and cook the other side for 30–60 seconds, or until cooked through.

3 Transfer the crêpe to a plate and keep hot. Repeat with the remaining batter, stacking the cooked crêpes on top of each other with waxed paper in between. Keep warm in the oven while cooking the remainder. Divide the filling between the crêpes, then roll up and dust with confectioners' sugar. Serve.

chocolate ginger pudding

ingredients

SERVES 4

3¹/₂ oz/100 g/generous
 ¹/₃ cup soft margarine
3¹/₂ oz/100 g/³/₄ cup
 self-rising flour, sifted
3¹/₂ oz/100 g/¹/₂ cup
 superfine sugar
2 eggs
1 oz/25 g/¹/₄ cup
 unsweetened cocoa, sifted
1 oz/25 g semisweet
 chocolate
1³/₄ oz/50 g preserved ginger

chocolate sauce

2 egg yolks
1 tbsp superfine sugar
1 tbsp cornstarch
10 fl oz/300 g/1¹/₄ cups milk
3¹/₂ oz/100 g semisweet
 chocolate, broken
 into pieces
confectioners' sugar,
 for dusting

method

1 Lightly grease 4 small individual ovenproof bowls. Place the margarine, flour, sugar, eggs, and cocoa in a mixing bowl and beat until well combined and smooth. Chop the chocolate and preserved ginger and stir into the mixture, ensuring they are well combined.

2 Divide the cake mixture between the prepared bowls and smooth the tops. Cover the bowls with disks of baking parchment and cover with a pleated sheet of foil. Cook the mini chocolate gingers in a steamer for 45 minutes until the sponges are cooked and springy to the touch.

3 Meanwhile, make the sauce. Beat the egg yolks, sugar, and cornstarch together to form a smooth paste. Heat the milk until boiling and pour over the egg mixture. Return to the pan and cook over very low heat, stirring until thick. Remove from the heat and beat in the chocolate. Stir until the chocolate melts.

4 Lift the chocolate gingers from the steamer, run a knife around the edge of the bowls, and carefully turn out onto serving plates. Dust each chocolate ginger with sugar and drizzle chocolate sauce over the top. Serve the remaining chocolate sauce separately.

sticky chocolate pudding

ingredients

SERVES 6

4¹/₂ oz/125 g/¹/₂ cup butter,
    softened
5¹/₂ oz/150 g/1 cup
    brown sugar
3 eggs, beaten
pinch of salt
1 oz/25 g/¹/₄ cup
    unsweetened cocoa
4¹/₂ oz/125 g/1 cup
    self-rising flour
1 oz/25 g semisweet
    chocolate, chopped finely
2³/₄ oz/75 g white chocolate,
    chopped finely

sauce

5 fl oz/150 ml/²/₃ cup
    heavy cream
2³/₄ oz/75 g/¹/₂ cup brown
    sugar
2 tbsp butter

method

1 Lightly grease 6 individual 6-fl oz/175-ml/
³/₄-cup individual dessert molds.

2 Cream the butter and sugar together in a
bowl until pale and fluffy. Beat in the eggs a
little at a time, beating well after each addition.
Sift the salt, cocoa, and flour into the creamed
mixture, and fold. Stir in the chopped
chocolate until evenly combined throughout.

3 Divide the mixture between the prepared
molds. Lightly grease 6 squares of foil and use
them to cover the tops of the molds, pressing
around the edges to seal. Place the molds in a
roasting pan and pour in boiling water to come
halfway up the sides of the molds. Bake in a
preheated oven, 350°F/180°C, for 50 minutes
or until a skewer inserted into the center of the
sponges comes out clean. Remove the molds
from the roasting pan and set aside.

4 To make the sauce, put the cream, sugar,
and butter into a pan and bring to a boil
over gentle heat. Simmer gently until the
sugar has completely dissolved, then transfer
to a warm pitcher.

5 To serve, run a knife around the edge of
each sponge, then turn out onto serving plates.
Serve immediately with the pitcher of sauce for
pouring over.

individual
chocolate pudding

ingredients

SERVES 4

pudding

3¹/2 oz/100 g/¹/2 cup
    superfine sugar
3 eggs
2³/4 oz/75 g/¹/2 cup
    all-purpose flour
1³/4 oz/50 g/¹/2 cup
    unsweetened cocoa
3¹/2 oz/100 g/scant ¹/2 cup
    unsalted butter, melted,
    plus extra for greasing
3¹/2 oz/100 g semisweet
    chocolate, melted

chocolate sauce

2 tbsp unsalted butter
3¹/2 oz/100 g semisweet
    chocolate
5 tbsp water
1 tbsp superfine sugar
1 tbsp coffee-flavored liqueur,
    such as Kahlua
coffee beans, to decorate

method

1 To make the desserts, put the sugar and eggs into a heatproof bowl and place over a pan of simmering water. Whisk for about 10 minutes until frothy. Remove the bowl from the heat and fold in the flour and cocoa. Fold in the butter, then the chocolate. Mix well. Grease 4 small heatproof bowls with butter. Spoon the mixture into the bowls and cover with waxed paper. Top with foil and secure with string. Place in a large pan filled with enough simmering water to reach halfway up the sides of the bowls. Steam for about 40 minutes, or until cooked through.

2 About 2–3 minutes before the end of the cooking time, make the sauce. Put the butter, chocolate, water, and sugar into a small pan and warm over low heat, stirring constantly, until melted together. Stir in the liqueur.

3 Remove the desserts from the heat, turn out into serving dishes, and pour over the sauce. Decorate with coffee beans and serve.

cappuccino soufflé pudding

ingredients

SERVES 6

butter, for greasing

2 tbsp golden superfine sugar,
     plus extra for coating

6 tbsp whipping cream

2 tsp instant espresso coffee
     granules

2 tbsp Kahlua

3 large eggs, separated,
     plus 1 extra egg white

5^1/$_2$ oz/150 g semisweet
     chocolate, melted
     and cooled

unsweetened cocoa,
     for dusting

chocolate-coated cookies,
     to serve

method

1 Lightly grease the sides of 6 x 6-fl oz/ 175-ml/^{3}/$_4$-cup ramekins with butter and coat with superfine sugar. Place the ramekins on a cookie sheet.

2 Place the cream in a small, heavy-bottom pan and heat gently. Stir in the coffee until it has dissolved, then stir in the Kahlua. Divide the coffee mixture between the prepared ramekins.

3 Place the egg whites in a clean, greasefree bowl and whisk until soft peaks form, then gradually whisk in the sugar until stiff but not dry. Stir the egg yolks and melted chocolate together in a separate bowl, then stir in a little of the whisked egg whites. Gradually fold in the remaining egg whites.

4 Divide the mixture between the dishes. Bake in a preheated oven, 375°F/190°C, for 15 minutes, or until just set. Dust with unsweetened cocoa and serve immediately with chocolate-coated cookies.

chocolate zabaglione

ingredients

SERVES 4

4 egg yolks

4 tbsp superfine sugar

1³/4 oz/50 g semisweet
   chocolate

4 fl oz/125 ml/¹/2 cup
   Marsala wine

unsweetened cocoa,
   for dusting

amaretti cookies, to serve

method

1 Place the egg yolks and superfine sugar in a large glass bowl and, using an electric whisk, whisk together until the mixture is very pale.

2 Grate the chocolate finely and, using a spatula, fold into the egg mixture. Fold the Marsala wine into the chocolate mixture.

3 Place the bowl over a pan of gently simmering water and set the electric whisk on the lowest speed or swap to a balloon whisk. Cook gently, whisking constantly, until the mixture thickens. Do not overcook or the mixture will curdle.

4 Spoon the hot mixture into 4 warmed glass dishes or coffee cups and dust with cocoa. Serve as soon as possible, while it is warm, light, and fluffy, with amaretti cookies.

chocolate fondue

ingredients

SERVES 6

1 pineapple

1 mango

12 cape gooseberries

9 oz/250 g/generous 1 cup
  fresh strawberries

9 oz/250 g/generous
  1^1/$_2$ cups seeded
  green grapes

fondue

9 oz/250 g semisweet
  chocolate, broken
  into pieces

5 fl oz/150 ml/^{2}/$_3$ cup
  heavy cream

2 tbsp brandy

method

1 Using a sharp knife, peel and core the pineapple, then cut the flesh into cubes. Peel the mango and cut the flesh into cubes. Peel back the papery outer skin of the cape gooseberries and twist at the top to make a "handle." Arrange all the fruit on 6 serving plates and let chill in the refrigerator.

2 To make the fondue, place the chocolate and cream in a fondue pot. Heat gently, stirring constantly, until the chocolate has melted. Stir in the brandy until thoroughly blended and the chocolate mixture is smooth.

3 Place the fondue pot over the burner to keep warm. To serve, allow each guest to dip the fruit into the sauce, using fondue forks or bamboo skewers.

chilled & iced desserts

Chilled and iced chocolate desserts have a wow factor that is hard to beat. Not suprisingly, most of them involve a generous quantity of cream as well as chocolate, making them even more heavenly! If you love the fluffy texture of mousse, aim for the chocolate terrine—there are three layers of mousse in milk, white, and semisweet chocolate—and if cheesecake is your passion, there's a great choice in this chapter.

The chapter begins with some gorgeous ice-cream recipes. Home-made ice cream is very easy to make, especially if you have an ice-cream maker, and once you have made your own you will never want to buy commercial ice cream again.

If you do not have an ice-cream maker and don't want to invest in one, you can still make perfect ice cream. Before you begin, set the freezer to its lowest temperature. Pour the prepared ice-cream mixture into a freezerproof container, uncovered, and freeze for 1–2 hours. When it starts to set around the edges, remove it from the freezer, turn it out into a bowl, and stir it with a fork or beat in an electric mixer until smooth. Add any extra ingredients at this point. Return to the freezer and freeze for an additional 2–3 hours, or until firm. Cover the container with a lid for storing. Transfer the ice cream to the refrigerator about 30 minutes before serving.

chocolate praline ice cream

ingredients

SERVES 4–6

3 oz/85 g semisweet chocolate, broken into pieces

10 fl oz/300 ml/1^{1}/$_{4}$ cups whole milk

10 oz/275 g/scant 1^{1}/$_{2}$ cup superfine sugar

3 egg yolks

10 fl oz/300 ml/1^{1}/$_{4}$ cups heavy whipping cream

praline

3^{1}/$_{2}$ oz/100 g/^{1}/$_{2}$ cup granulated sugar

2 tbsp water

2 oz/55 g/scant ^{1}/$_{3}$ cup blanched almonds

vegetable oil, for oiling

method

1 To prepare the praline, put the sugar, water, and nuts in a large heavy-bottom pan and heat gently, stirring, to dissolve the sugar. Let the mixture bubble gently, without stirring, for 6–10 minutes, until lightly golden brown, then immediately pour it onto an oiled cookie sheet and spread it out evenly. Let cool for 1 hour, or until cold and hardened, then place it in a plastic bag and crush with a hammer.

2 To make the ice cream, put the chocolate and milk in a pan and heat gently, stirring, until the chocolate has melted and the mixture is smooth. Remove from the heat.

3 Whisk the sugar and egg yolks together in a large bowl until pale and the mixture leaves a trail when the whisk is lifted. Slowly add the milk mixture, stirring constantly with a wooden spoon. Strain the mixture into the rinsed-out pan and cook over low heat for 10–15 minutes, stirring all the time, until the mixture thickens enough to coat the back of the spoon. Do not let the mixture boil or it will curdle.

4 Remove the sauce from the heat and let cool for at least 1 hour, stirring from time to time to prevent a skin forming. Whip the cream until it holds its shape, then fold in the cold sauce and churn the mixture in an ice-cream maker. Just before the ice cream freezes, add the praline and churn to mix.

marbled chocolate & orange ice cream

ingredients

SERVES 6

6 oz/175 g white chocolate

1 tsp cornstarch

1 tsp vanilla extract

3 egg yolks

10 fl oz/300 ml/1$\frac{1}{4}$ cups milk

16 fl oz/450 ml/2 cups
    heavy cream

4 oz/115 g orange-flavored
    semisweet chocolate,
    broken into pieces

grated orange rind,
    to decorate

orange segments, to serve

method

1 Using a sharp knife, chop the white chocolate into small pieces and set aside. Beat the cornstarch, vanilla extract, and egg yolks in a heatproof bowl until well blended. Pour the milk into a large, heavy-bottom pan and bring to a boil over low heat. Pour over the egg yolk mixture, stirring constantly.

2 Strain the mixture back into the pan and heat gently, stirring constantly, until thickened. Remove from the heat, add the white chocolate pieces and stir until melted. Stir in the cream. Set aside 6 fl oz/150 ml/ $\frac{2}{3}$ cup of the mixture and pour the remainder into a large freezerproof container. Cover and freeze for 2 hours, or until starting to set. Melt the orange-flavored chocolate, stir into the reserved mixture and set aside.

3 Remove the partially frozen ice cream from the freezer and beat with a fork. Place spoonfuls of the orange chocolate mixture over the ice cream and swirl with a knife to give a marbled effect. Freeze for 8 hours, or overnight, until firm. Transfer to the refrigerator 30 minutes before serving. Scoop into individual glasses, decorate with orange rind, and serve with a few orange segments.

rich chocolate ice cream

ingredients

SERVES 6
ice cream

1 egg

3 egg yolks

3 oz/85 g/scant ¹/₂ cup
   superfine sugar

10 fl oz/300 ml/1¹/₄ cups
   whole milk

9 oz/250 g semisweet
   chocolate

10 fl oz/250 g/1¹/₄ cups
   heavy cream

trellis cups

3¹/₂ oz/100 g semisweet
   chocolate

method

1 Beat the egg, egg yolks, and superfine sugar together in a mixing bowl until well combined. Heat the milk until it is almost boiling. Gradually pour the hot milk onto the eggs, whisking. Place the bowl over a pan of gently simmering water and cook, stirring constantly, until the custard mixture thickens sufficiently to thinly coat the back of a wooden spoon.

2 Break the chocolate into small pieces and add to the hot custard. Stir until the chocolate has melted. Cover with a sheet of dampened baking parchment and let cool.

3 Whip the cream until just holding its shape, then fold into the cooled chocolate custard. Transfer to a freezerproof container and freeze for 1–2 hours until the mixture is frozen 1 inch/2.5 cm from the sides. Scrape the ice cream into a chilled bowl and beat again until smooth. Re-freeze until firm.

4 To make the trellis cups, invert a muffin pan and cover 6 alternate mounds with plastic wrap. Melt the chocolate, place it in a paper pastry bag, and snip off the end.

5 Pipe a circle around the bottom of the mound, then pipe chocolate back and forth over it to form a double-thickness trellis. Pipe around the bottom again. Chill until set, then lift from the pan and remove the plastic wrap. Serve the ice cream in the trellis cups.

chocolate chip & fudge banana ice cream

ingredients

SERVES 6

4 ripe bananas

juice of $^1/_2$ lemon

7 oz/200 g/1 cup golden
   superfine sugar

18 fl oz/500 ml/generous
   2 cups whipping cream

3$^1/_2$ oz/100 g/generous
   $^1/_2$ cup semisweet
   chocolate chips

3$^1/_2$ oz/100 g fudge, cut into
   small pieces, plus extra
   to decorate

method

1 Peel the bananas and chop them coarsely, then place in a food processor with the lemon juice and sugar. Process until well chopped, then pour in the cream and process again until well blended.

2 Freeze in an ice-cream maker, following the manufacturer's instructions, adding the chocolate chips and fudge just before the ice cream is ready.

3 Transfer the ice cream to the refrigerator 15 minutes before serving. Scoop into small bowls and decorate with extra fudge pieces. Serve.

coconut & white chocolate ice cream

ingredients

SERVES 6

2 eggs

2 egg yolks

4 oz/115 g/generous $^1/_2$ cup golden superfine sugar

10 fl oz/300 ml/1$^1/_4$ cups light cream

4 oz/115 g white chocolate, chopped

4 oz/115 g creamed coconut, chopped

10 fl oz/300 ml/1$^1/_4$ cups heavy cream

3 tbsp coconut rum

tropical fruit, such as mango, pineapple, or passion fruit, to serve

method

1 Place the whole eggs, egg yolks, and sugar in a heatproof bowl and beat together until well blended. Place the light cream, chocolate, and coconut in a pan and heat gently until the chocolate has melted, then continue to heat, stirring constantly, until almost boiling. Pour onto the egg mixture, stirring vigorously, then set the bowl over a pan of gently simmering water, making sure that the base of the bowl does not touch the water.

2 Heat the mixture, stirring constantly, until it lightly coats the back of the spoon. Strain into a clean, heatproof bowl and let cool. Place the heavy cream and rum in a separate bowl and whip until slightly thickened, then fold into the cooled chocolate mixture.

3 Freeze in an ice-cream maker, following the manufacturer's instructions. Transfer the ice cream to the refrigerator for 30 minutes before serving. Scoop into small serving bowls and serve with tropical fruit.

white chocolate ice cream

ingredients

SERVES 6

ice cream

1 egg, plus 1 extra egg yolk

3 tbsp superfine sugar

5^1/$_2$ oz/150 g white chocolate

10 fl oz/300 ml/1^1/$_4$ cups milk

5 fl oz/150 ml/^{2}/$_3$ cup
   heavy cream

cookie cups

1 egg white

4 tbsp superfine sugar

2 tbsp all-purpose flour, sifted

2 tbsp unsweetened cocoa,
   sifted

2 tbsp butter, melted

semisweet chocolate, melted,
   to serve

method

1 Line 2 cookie sheets with baking parchment. To make the ice cream, beat the egg, egg yolk, and sugar. Break the chocolate into pieces, place in a bowl with 3 tablespoons of milk, and melt over a pan of hot water. Heat the milk until almost boiling and pour onto the eggs, whisking. Place over a pan of simmering water and stir until the mixture thickens. Whisk in the chocolate. Cover with dampened baking parchment and let cool.

2 Whip the cream and fold into the custard. Transfer to a freezerproof container and freeze the mixture for 1–2 hours. Scrape into a bowl and beat until smooth. Re-freeze until firm.

3 To make the cookie cups, beat the egg white and sugar. Beat in the flour and cocoa, then the butter. Place 1 tablespoon on 1 cookie sheet and spread out into a 5-inch/ 12^1/$_2$-cm circle. Bake in a preheated oven, 400°F/ 200°C, for 4–5 minutes. Remove and mold over an upturned cup. Let set, then cool. Repeat to make 6 cookie cups. Serve the ice cream in the cups, drizzled with melted chocolate.

sicilian cassata

ingredients

SERVES 8

5¹/2 oz/150 g/generous 1 cup
self-rising flour
2 tbsp unsweetened cocoa
1 tsp baking powder
6 oz/175 g butter, softened,
plus extra for greasing
6 oz/175 g/scant 1 cup
golden superfine sugar
3 eggs
confectioners' sugar,
for dusting
chocolate curls, to decorate

filling

1 lb/450 g ricotta cheese
3¹/2 oz/100 g semisweet
chocolate, grated
4 oz/115 g/generous ¹/2 cup
golden superfine sugar
3 tbsp Marsala wine
2 oz/55 g/¹/3 cup chopped
candied peel
2 tbsp almonds, chopped

method

1 Sift the flour, unsweetened cocoa, and baking powder into a large bowl. Add the butter, sugar, and eggs and beat together thoroughly until smooth and creamy. Pour the cake batter into a greased and base-lined 7-inch/18-cm round cake pan and bake in a preheated oven, 375°F/190°C, for 30–40 minutes, or until well risen and firm to the touch. Let stand in the pan for 5 minutes, then turn out onto a wire rack to cool completely.

2 Wash and dry the cake pan and grease and line it again. To make the filling, rub the ricotta through a strainer into a bowl. Add the grated chocolate, sugar, and Marsala wine and beat together until the mixture is light and fluffy. Stir in the candied peel and almonds.

3 Cut the thin crust off the top of the cake and discard. Cut the cake horizontally into 3 layers. Place the first slice in the prepared pan and cover with half the ricotta mixture. Repeat the layers, finishing with a cake layer. Press down lightly, cover with a plate and a weight, and let chill in the refrigerator for 8 hours, or overnight. To serve, turn the cake out onto a serving plate. Dust with confectioners' sugar and decorate with chocolate curls.

zucotto

ingredients

SERVES 6

4 oz/115 g soft margarine,
    plus extra for greasing
3 1/2 oz/100 g/scant 2/3 cup
    self-rising flour
2 tbsp unsweetened cocoa
1/2 tsp baking powder
4 oz/115 g/generous 1/2 cup
    golden superfine sugar
2 eggs, beaten
3 tbsp brandy
2 tbsp Kirsch

filling

10 fl oz/300 ml/1 1/4 cups
    heavy cream
1 oz/25 g/1/4 cup
    confectioners' sugar, sifted
2 oz/55 g/1/4 cup toasted
    almonds, chopped
8 oz/225 g black cherries,
    pitted
2 oz/55 g semisweet chocolate,
    finely chopped

to decorate

1 tbsp unsweetened cocoa
1 tbsp confectioners' sugar
fresh cherries

method

1 Grease a 12 x 9-inch/30 x 23-cm jelly roll pan with margarine and line with parchment paper. Sift the flour, cocoa, and baking powder into a bowl. Add the sugar, margarine, and eggs. Beat together until well mixed, then spoon into the prepared pan. Bake in a preheated oven, 375°F/190°C, for 15–20 minutes, or until well risen and firm to the touch. Let stand in the pan for 5 minutes, then turn out onto a wire rack to cool.

2 Using the rim of a 2 1/2 pint/1.2-liter/5-cup ovenproof bowl as a guide, cut a circle from the cake and set aside. Line the bowl with plastic wrap. Use the remaining cake, cutting it as necessary, to line the bowl. Place the brandy and Kirsch in a small bowl and mix together. Sprinkle over the cake, including the reserved circle.

3 To make the filling, pour the cream into a separate bowl and add the confectioners' sugar. Whip until thick, then fold in the almonds, cherries, and chocolate. Fill the sponge mold with the cream mixture and press the cake circle on top. Cover with a plate and a weight, and let chill in the refrigerator for 6–8 hours, or overnight. When ready to serve, turn the zucotto out onto a serving plate. Decorate with cocoa and confectioners' sugar, sifted over in alternating segments, and a few cherries.

iced white chocolate terrine

ingredients

SERVES 8

2 tbsp granulated sugar

5 tbsp water

$10^{1}/_{2}$ oz/300 g white
chocolate

3 eggs, separated

10 fl oz/300 ml/$1^{1}/_{4}$ cups
heavy cream

strawberry coulis and fresh
strawberries, to serve

method

1 Line a 1-lb/450-g loaf pan with foil or plastic wrap, pressing out as many creases as you can.

2 Place the granulated sugar and water in a heavy-based pan and heat gently, stirring until the sugar has dissolved. Bring to a boil, then boil for 1–2 minutes until syrupy. Remove the pan from the heat.

3 Break the white chocolate into small pieces and stir it into the syrup, continuing to stir until the chocolate has melted and combined with the syrup. Let cool slightly. Beat the egg yolks into the chocolate mixture. Set aside to cool completely.

4 Lightly whip the cream until just holding its shape, and fold it into the chocolate mixture. Whisk the egg whites in a clean bowl until they are standing in soft peaks. Fold the whites into the chocolate mixture. Pour into the prepared loaf pan and freeze overnight.

5 To serve, remove the terrine from the freezer about 10–15 minutes before serving and remove the foil or plastic wrap. Turn out of the pan and cut into slices to serve.

champagne mousse

ingredients

SERVES 4

sponge

4 eggs

3^1/$_2$ oz/100 g/^{1}/$_2$ cup
   superfine sugar

2^3/$_4$ oz/75 g/^{2}/$_3$ cup
   self-rising flour

2 tbsp unsweetened cocoa

2 tbsp butter, melted

mousse

1 packaged powdered gelatin

3 tbsp water

10 fl oz/300 ml/1^1/$_4$ cups
   champagne

10 fl oz/300 ml/1^1/$_4$ cups
   heavy cream

2 egg whites

6 tbsp superfine sugar

to decorate

2 oz/50 g semisweet
   chocolate-flavored cake
   covering, melted

method

1 Line a 15 x 10-inch/38 x 25-cm jelly roll pan with greased baking parchment. Place the eggs and sugar in a bowl and beat, using an electric mixer, until the mixture is very thick and the whisk leaves a trail when lifted. Strain the flour and cocoa together and fold into the egg mixture. Fold in the butter. Pour into the pan and bake in a preheated oven, 400°F/200°C, for 8 minutes or until springy to the touch. Let cool for 5 minutes, then turn out onto a wire rack until cold. Meanwhile, line four 4-inch/10-cm baking rings with baking parchment. Line the sides with 1-inch/2.5-cm strips of cake and the bottom with circles.

2 For the mousse, sprinkle the gelatin over the water and let it go spongy. Place the bowl over a pan of hot water and stir until the gelatin has dissolved. Stir in the champagne.

3 Whip the cream until just holding its shape. Fold in the champagne mixture. Stand in a cool place until on the point of setting, stirring. Whisk the egg whites until standing in soft peaks, add the sugar and whisk until glossy. Carefully fold the egg whites into the setting mixture. Spoon into the sponge cases, allowing the mixture to go above the sponge. Let chill for 2 hours. Pipe the cake covering in squiggles on a piece of parchment, let them set, then use to decorate the mousses.

white chocolate mousse

ingredients

SERVES 6

9 oz/250 g white chocolate,
   broken into pieces

3^1/2 fl oz/100 ml/generous
   ^{1}/3 cup milk

10 fl oz/300 ml/1^1/4 cups
   heavy cream

1 tsp rose water

2 egg whites

4 oz/115 g semisweet
   chocolate, broken
   into pieces

candied rose petals,
   to decorate

method

1 Place the white chocolate and milk in a pan and heat gently until the chocolate has melted, then stir. Transfer to a large bowl and let cool.

2 Place the cream and rose water in a separate bowl and whip until soft peaks form. Whisk the egg whites in a separate spotlessly clean, greasefree bowl until stiff but not dry. Gently fold the whipped cream into the white chocolate, then fold in the egg whites. Spoon the mixture into 6 small dishes or glasses, cover with plastic wrap and let chill for 8 hours, or overnight, to set.

3 Melt the semisweet chocolate and let cool, then pour evenly over the mousses. Let stand until the chocolate has hardened, then decorate with rose petals and serve.

white chocolate molds

ingredients

SERVES 6

4¹/₂ oz/125 g white chocolate,
  broken into pieces
9 fl oz/250 ml/1 cup
  heavy cream
3 tbsp crème fraîche
2 eggs, separated
3 tbsp water
1¹/₂ tsp powdered gelatin
5 oz/140 g sliced strawberries
5 oz/140 g raspberries
5 oz/140 g black currants
5 tbsp superfine sugar
4 fl oz/125 ml/¹/₂ cup crème
  de framboise
12 black currant leaves,
  if available

method

1 Put the chocolate in a heatproof bowl set over a pan of barely simmering water. Stir over a low heat until melted and smooth. Remove from the heat and set aside.

2 Pour the cream into a pan and bring to just below boiling point over a low heat. Remove from the heat, then stir the cream and crème fraîche into the chocolate and let cool slightly. Beat in the egg yolks, one at a time.

3 Pour the water into bowl and sprinkle over the gelatin. Let stand for 2–3 minutes to soften, then set over a pan of barely simmering water until dissolved. Stir into the chocolate mixture and let stand until nearly set.

4 Brush the insides of 6 timbales or ramekins with oil and line the bases with parchment paper. Whisk the egg whites until soft peaks form, then fold them into the chocolate mixture. Divide the mixture among the molds and smooth the surface. Cover with plastic wrap and let chill for 2 hours, until set.

5 Put the strawberries, raspberries, and black currants in a bowl. Sprinkle with the superfine sugar, then gently stir in the liqueur. Cover with plastic wrap and let chill for 2 hours.

6 To serve, run a round-bladed knife around the molds and turn out onto individual plates. Divide the fruit among the plates and serve decorated with black currant leaves.

chocolate rum pots

ingredients

SERVES 6

8 oz/225 g semisweet
    chocolate

4 eggs, separated

6 tbsp superfine sugar

4 tbsp dark rum

4 tbsp heavy cream

to decorate

a little whipped cream
    (optional)

marbled chocolate shapes

method

1 Melt the semisweet chocolate and let cool slightly. Whisk the egg yolks with the superfine sugar in a bowl until very pale and fluffy. Drizzle the chocolate into the egg yolk and sugar mixture and fold in together with the dark rum and the heavy cream.

2 Whisk the egg whites in a clean bowl until standing in soft peaks. Fold the egg whites into the chocolate mixture in 2 batches. Divide the mixture among 6 individual dishes, and let chill for at least 2 hours before serving.

3 To serve, decorate with a little whipped cream if liked and a marbled chocolate shape.

chocolate & orange pots

ingredients

SERVES 6

7 oz/200 g plain chocolate,
  broken into pieces
grated rind of 1 orange
10 fl oz/300 ml/1¼ cups
  heavy cream
5 oz/140 g/¾ cup golden
  superfine sugar
3 tbsp Cointreau
3 large egg whites
fine strips of orange rind, to
  decorate
crisp biscuits, to serve

method

1 Melt the chocolate and stir in the orange rind. Place the cream in a bowl with 100 g/ 3½ oz of the sugar and the Cointreau and whip until thick.

2 Place the egg whites in a separate spotlessly clean, greasefree bowl and whisk until soft peaks form, then gradually whisk in the remaining sugar until stiff but not dry. Fold the melted chocolate into the cream, then beat in a spoonful of the whisked egg whites. Gently fold in the remaining egg whites until thoroughly mixed.

3 Spoon the mixture into 6 small ramekin dishes or demi-tasse coffee cups. Cover and leave to chill in the refrigerator for 1 hour, then decorate with a few strips of orange rind before serving with crisp biscuits.

chocolate & strawberry brûlées

ingredients

SERVES 6

9 oz/250 g/scant 1¹/₄ cups
    fresh strawberries, washed
    and hulled
2 tbsp fruit liqueur, such as
    Kirsch or crème de cassis
16 fl oz/450 ml/2 cups
    heavy cream
4 oz/115 g semisweet
    chocolate, melted
    and cooled
4 oz/115 g/¹/₂ cup firmly
    packed raw brown sugar

to decorate

fresh strawberries
fresh mint leaves

method

1 Cut the strawberries into halves or fourths, depending on their size, and divide among 6 ramekins. Sprinkle with the fruit liqueur.

2 Pour the cream into a bowl and whip until it is just holding its shape. Add the cooled chocolate and continue whipping until the cream is thick. Spread over the strawberries. Cover and place in the freezer for 2 hours, or until the cream is frozen.

3 Preheat the broiler to high. Sprinkle the sugar thickly over the cream, then place under the hot broiler and cook until the sugar has melted and caramelized. Let the brûlées stand for 30 minutes, or until the fruit and cream have thawed. Serve decorated with a few fresh strawberries and mint leaves.

coffee panna cotta with chocolate sauce

ingredients

SERVES 6

oil, for brushing

1 pint/600 ml/2^1/$_2$ cups
  heavy cream

1 vanilla pod

2 oz/55 g/^{1}/$_3$ cup golden
  superfine sugar

2 tsp instant espresso coffee
  granules, dissolved in
  4 tbsp water

2 tsp powdered gelatin

chocolate-covered coffee
  beans, to serve

sauce

5 fl oz/150 ml/^{2}/$_3$ cup
  light cream

2 oz/55 g semisweet
  chocolate, melted

method

1 Lightly brush 6 x 150-ml/5-fl oz molds with oil. Place the cream in a saucepan. Split the vanilla pod and scrape the black seeds into the cream. Add the vanilla pod and the sugar, then heat gently until almost boiling. Sieve the cream into a heatproof bowl and reserve. Place the coffee in a small heatproof bowl, sprinkle on the gelatin and leave for 5 minutes, or until spongy. Set the bowl over a saucepan of gently simmering water until the gelatin has dissolved.

2 Stir a little of the reserved cream into the gelatin mixture, then stir the gelatin mixture into the remainder of the cream. Divide the mixture among the prepared molds and let cool, then leave to chill in the refrigerator for 8 hours, or overnight.

3 To make the sauce, place one-quarter of the cream in a bowl and stir in the melted chocolate. Gradually stir in the remaining cream, reserving 1 tablespoon. To serve the panna cotta, dip the base of the molds briefly into hot water and turn out onto 6 dessert plates. Pour the chocolate cream around. Dot drops of the reserved cream onto the sauce and feather it with a skewer. Decorate with chocolate-covered coffee beans and serve.

chocolate coeurs à la crème

ingredients

SERVES 8

8 oz/225 g/generous 1 cup
   ricotta cheese

2oz/55 g/$^{1}/_{2}$ cup
   confectioners'
   sugar, sifted

10 fl oz/300 ml/1$^{1}/_{4}$ cups
   heavy cream

1 tsp vanilla extract

2 oz/55 g semisweet
   chocolate, grated

2 egg whites

coulis

8 oz/225 g/1 cup fresh
   raspberries

confectioners' sugar, to taste

to decorate

fresh strawberries, halved

fresh raspberries

method

1 Line 8 individual molds with cheesecloth. Press the ricotta cheese through a strainer into a bowl. Add the confectioners' sugar, cream, and vanilla extract and beat together thoroughly. Stir in the grated chocolate. Place the egg whites in a separate clean bowl and whisk until stiff but not dry. Gently fold into the cheese mixture.

2 Spoon the mixture into the prepared molds. Stand the molds on a tray or dish and let drain in the refrigerator for 8 hours, or overnight—the cheesecloth will absorb most of the liquid.

3 To make the raspberry coulis, place the raspberries in a food processor and process to a purée. Press the purée through a strainer into a bowl and add confectioners' sugar, to taste. To serve, turn each dessert out onto a serving plate and pour the raspberry coulis round. Decorate with strawberries and raspberries, then serve.

chocolate marquise

ingredients

SERVES 6

7 oz/200 g semisweet
   chocolate
3¹/₂ oz/100 g/generous
   ¹/₃ cup butter
3 egg yolks
2³/₄ oz/75 g/¹/₃ cup
   superfine sugar
1 tsp chocolate extract or
   1 tbsp chocolate-flavored
   liqueur
10 fl oz/300 ml/1¹/₄ cups
   heavy cream

to serve

crème fraîche
chocolate-dipped fruits
unsweetened cocoa,
   for dusting

method

1 Break the chocolate into pieces. Place the chocolate and butter in a bowl set over a pan of gently simmering water and stir until melted and well combined. Remove the pan from the heat and let the chocolate cool.

2 Place the egg yolks in a mixing bowl with the sugar and whisk until pale and fluffy. Using an electric mixer running on low speed, slowly whisk in the cool chocolate mixture. Stir in the chocolate extract or chocolate-flavored liqueur.

3 Whip the cream until just holding its shape. Fold into the chocolate mixture. Spoon into 6 small custard pots or individual metal molds. Chill the desserts for at least 2 hours.

4 To serve, turn out the desserts onto individual serving dishes. If you have difficulty turning them out, first dip the pots or molds into a bowl of warm water for a few seconds. Serve with chocolate-dipped fruit and crème fraîche and dust with cocoa.

marble cheesecake

ingredients

SERVES 10

base

8 oz/225 g toasted oat cereal

1³/₄ oz/50 g/¹/₂ cup toasted
hazelnuts, chopped

4 tbsp butter

1 oz/25 g semisweet chocolate

filling

12 oz/350 g full-fat soft cheese

3¹/₂ oz/100 g/¹/₂ cup
superfine sugar

7 fl oz/200 ml/generous
³/₄ cup thick yogurt

10 fl oz/300 ml/1¹/₄ cups
heavy cream

1 packaged powdered gelatin

3 tbsp water

6 oz/175 g semisweet
chocolate, melted

6 oz/175 g white chocolate,
melted

method

1 Place the toasted oat cereal in a plastic bag and crush it coarsely with a rolling pin. Pour the crushed cereal into a mixing bowl and stir in the toasted chopped hazelnuts.

2 Melt the butter and chocolate together over low heat and stir into the cereal mixture, stirring until well coated.

3 Using the bottom of a glass, press the mixture into the bottom and up the sides of an 8-inch/ 20-cm springform cake pan.

4 Beat the cheese and sugar together with a wooden spoon until smooth. Beat in the yogurt. Whip the cream until just holding its shape and fold into the mixture. Sprinkle the gelatin over the water in a heatproof bowl and let it go spongy. Place over a pan of hot water and stir until dissolved. Stir into the mixture.

5 Divide the mixture in half and beat the semisweet chocolate into one half and the white chocolate into the other half.

6 Place alternate spoonfuls of mixture on top of the cereal base. Swirl the filling together with the tip of a knife to give a marbled effect. Smooth the top with a scraper or a spatula. Chill the cheesecake for at least 2 hours, until set, before serving.

irish cream cheesecake

ingredients

SERVES 12

oil, for brushing

6 oz/175 g chocolate chip
   cookies

2 oz/55 g butter

filling

8 oz/225 g semisweet
   chocolate

8 oz/225 g milk chocolate

2 oz/55 g/^{3}/$_4$ cup golden
   superfine sugar

12 oz/350 g/1^1/$_2$ cups
   cream cheese

15 fl oz/425 ml/1^3/$_4$ cups
   heavy cream, whipped

3 tbsp Irish cream liqueur

crème fraîche or sour cream

fresh fruit, to serve

method

1 Line the base of a 20-cm/8-inch springform tin with foil and brush the sides with oil. Place the cookies in a polythene bag and crush with a rolling pin. Place the butter in a saucepan and heat gently until just melted, then stir in the crushed biscuits. Press the mixture into the base of the tin and chill in the refrigerator for 1 hour.

2 To make the filling, melt the semisweet and milk chocolate together, stir to combine and leave to cool. Place the sugar and cream cheese in a large bowl and beat together until smooth, then fold in the whipped cream. Fold the mixture gently into the melted chocolate, then stir in the Irish cream liqueur.

3 Spoon the filling over the chilled biscuit base and smooth the surface. Cover and leave to chill in the refrigerator for 2 hours, or until quite firm. Transfer to a serving plate and cut into small slices. Serve with a spoonful of crème fraîche and fresh fruit.

banana coconut cheesecake

ingredients

SERVES 10

8 oz/225 g chocolate chip
   cookies

4 tbsp butter

12 oz/350 g medium-fat
   soft cheese

$2^3/4$ oz/75 g/$^1/3$ cup
   superfine sugar

$1^3/4$ oz/50 g fresh coconut,
   grated

2 tbsp coconut-flavored
   liqueur

2 ripe bananas

$4^1/2$ oz/125 g semisweet
   chocolate

1 packaged powdered gelatin

3 tbsp water

5 fl oz/150 ml/$^2/3$ cup
   heavy cream

to decorate

1 banana

lemon juice

a little melted chocolate

method

1 Place the cookies in a plastic bag and crush with a rolling pin. Pour into a mixing bowl. Melt the butter and stir into the cookie crumbs until well coated. Firmly press the cookie mixture into the bottom and up the sides of an 8-inch/ 20-cm springform cake pan.

2 Beat the soft cheese and superfine sugar together until well combined, then beat in the grated coconut and coconut-flavored liqueur. Mash the 2 bananas and beat them in. Melt the semisweet chocolate and beat in until well combined.

3 Sprinkle the gelatin over the water in a heatproof bowl and let it go spongy. Place over a pan of hot water and stir until dissolved. Stir into the chocolate mixture. Whip the cream until just holding its shape and stir into the chocolate mixture. Spoon the filling over the biscuit shell and let chill for 2 hours, until set.

4 To serve, carefully transfer to a serving plate. Slice the banana, toss in the lemon juice, and arrange around the edge of the cheesecake. Drizzle with melted chocolate and let set before serving.

chocolate terrine with orange cream

ingredients

SERVES 10–12

6 tbsp water

3 tsp powdered gelatin

4 oz/115 g each of milk, white, and semisweet chocolate, broken into pieces

16 fl oz/450 ml/2 cups whipping cream

6 eggs, separated

2³/₄ oz/75 g/scant ³/₈ cup superfine sugar

orange cream

2 tbsp superfine sugar

1 tbsp cornstarch

2 egg yolks

5 fl oz/150 ml/²/₃ cup milk

5 fl oz/150 ml/²/₃ cup heavy cream

grated rind of 1 orange

1 tbsp Cointreau

to decorate

5 fl oz/150 ml/²/₃ cup heavy cream, whipped

chocolate-covered coffee beans

orange zest

method

1 To make the milk chocolate mousse, place 2 tablespoons of the water in a heatproof bowl. Sprinkle on 1 teaspoon of gelatin and let stand for 5 minutes. Set the bowl over a pan of simmering water until the gelatin has dissolved. Let cool. Melt the milk chocolate and let cool. Whip one-third of the cream until thick. Whisk 2 of the egg whites in a bowl until stiff but not dry. Whisk 2 of the egg yolks and one-third of the sugar in a separate bowl until thick. Stir in the chocolate, gelatin, and whipped cream. Fold in the whisked egg whites.

2 Pour into a 2³/₄-pint/1.2-liter/5-cup loaf pan, lined with plastic wrap. Cover and freeze for 20 minutes, or until set. Make the white chocolate mousse in the same way, pour over the milk chocolate mousse and freeze. Make the semisweet chocolate mousse and pour on top. Chill for 2 hours, until set.

3 To make the orange cream, stir the sugar, cornstarch, and egg yolks together until smooth. Heat the milk, cream, and orange rind in a pan until almost boiling, then pour over the egg mixture, whisking. Strain back into the pan and heat until thick. Cover and let cool, then stir in the Cointreau. Turn out the terrine. Decorate with cream, coffee beans, and orange zest. Serve with the orange cream.

chocolate & cherry tiramisù

ingredients

SERVES 4

200 ml/7 fl oz/generous
   ³/4 cup strong black
   coffee, cooled to room
   temperature
6 tbsp cherry brandy
16 trifle sponges
9 oz/250 g/1¹/4 cups
   mascarpone
10 fl oz/300 ml/1¹/4 cups
   heavy cream,
   lightly whipped
3 tbsp confectioner's sugar
9¹/2 oz/275 g sweet cherries,
   halved and pitted
2¹/4 oz/60 g chocolate,
   curls or grated
whole cherries, to decorate

method

1 Pour the cooled coffee into a pitcher and stir in the cherry brandy. Put half of the trifle sponges into the bottom of a serving dish, then pour over half of the coffee mixture.

2 Put the mascarpone into a separate bowl along with the cream and sugar, and mix together well. Spread half of the mascarpone mixture over the coffee-soaked trifle sponges, then top with half of the cherries. Arrange the remaining trifle sponges on top. Pour over the remaining coffee mixture and top with the remaining cherries. Finish with a layer of mascarpone mixture. Scatter over the grated chocolate, cover with plastic wrap, and chill in the refrigerator for at least 2 hours.

3 Remove from the refrigerator, decorate with cherries, and serve.

chocolate trifle

ingredients

SERVES 4

10 oz/280 g ready-made
   chocolate loaf cake
3–4 tbsp seeded raspberry
   jelly
4 tbsp amaretto liqueur
9 oz/250 g package frozen
   mixed red fruit, thawed

custard

6 egg yolks
2 oz/55 g/generous 1/4 cup
   golden superfine sugar
1 tbsp cornstarch
18 fl oz/500 ml/2 cups milk
2 oz/55 g semisweet
   chocolate, melted

topping

8 fl oz/225 ml/1 cup
   heavy cream
1 tbsp golden superfine sugar
1/2 tsp vanilla extract

to decorate

ready-made chocolate truffles
fresh fruit, such as cherries
   and strawberries

method

1 Cut the cake into slices and make "sandwiches" with the raspberry jelly. Cut the sandwiches into cubes and place in a large serving bowl. Sprinkle with the amaretto liqueur. Spread the fruit over the cake.

2 To make the custard, place the egg yolks and sugar in a heatproof bowl and whisk until thick and pale, then stir in the cornstarch. Place the milk in a pan and heat until almost boiling. Pour onto the egg yolk mixture, stirring. Return the mixture to the pan and bring just to a boil, stirring constantly, until it thickens. Remove from the heat and let cool slightly. Stir in the melted chocolate. Pour the custard over the cake and fruit. Let cool, then cover and let chill in the refrigerator for 2 hours, or until set.

3 To make the topping, whip the cream until soft peaks form, then beat in the sugar and vanilla extract. Spoon over the trifle. Decorate with the truffles and fruit and let chill until ready to serve.

cakes & tortes

This chapter starts with a devil's food cake, a hint of wickedness that sets the tone for all the other recipes. There is no point in pretending that these delicious cakes and tortes are anything less than pure, unadulterated indulgence, although if you think a hint of fruit or vegetables might lend a slightly virtuous air, you could try the date and chocolate cake or the chocolate passion cake! Be warned, however—the grated carrots in the passion cake only serve to make it irresistibly moist, so you probably won't be able to resist a second slice.

There's a decidedly grown-up feel to most of the cakes in this selection, and indeed many of them would make a stylish dessert to end an elegant dinner party—the mocha layer cake, perhaps, or the chocolate truffle torte. Your guests will love you!

So that the young ones don't feel left out, though, there's a lovely family chocolate cake, ideal for Sunday afternoon tea. There are some pretty little cupcakes, too, which would be perfect served at a children's party—with plenty of napkins at hand for mopping up, because they are delightfully messy to eat. In the middle of each warm, molten-centered cupcake is a square of pure chocolate, which spills out when you bite into it. Mmm!

devil's food cake

ingredients

SERVES 10–12

3¹/₂ oz/100 g semisweet
   chocolate
9 oz/250 g/generous
   1⁵/₈ cups self-rising flour
1 tsp baking soda
8 oz/225 g butter, plus extra
   for greasing
14 oz/400 g/2 cups firmly
   packed dark brown sugar
1 tsp vanilla extract
3 eggs
4 fl oz/125 ml/¹/₂ cup
   buttermilk
8 fl oz/225 ml/1 cup
   boiling water

frosting

10¹/₂ oz/300 g/1¹/₂ cups
   superfine sugar
2 egg whites
1 tbsp lemon juice
3 tbsp orange juice
candied orange peel,
   to decorate

method

1 Melt the chocolate in a heatproof bowl over a pan of simmering water. Sift the flour and baking soda together.

2 Place the butter and sugar in a large bowl and beat until pale and fluffy. Beat in the vanilla extract and the eggs, one at a time, beating well after each addition. Add a little flour if the mixture starts to curdle. Fold the melted chocolate into the mixture until well blended. Fold in the remaining flour, then stir in the buttermilk and 8 fl oz/225 ml/1 cup boiling water.

3 Divide the mixture between 2 lightly greased and base-lined 8-inch/20-cm shallow round cake pans and level the tops. Bake in a preheated oven, 375°F/190°C, for 30 minutes, or until springy to the touch. Let cool in the pan for 5 minutes, then transfer to a wire rack and let cool completely.

4 Place the frosting ingredients in a large bowl set over a pan of simmering water. Using an electric whisk, whisk until thick and forming soft peaks. Remove from the heat and whisk until the mixture is cool.

5 Sandwich the 2 cakes together with a little of the frosting, then spread the remainder over the sides and top of the cake. Decorate with candied orange peel.

mocha layer cake

ingredients

SERVES 8

butter for greasing

7 oz/200 g/generous
    1¼ cups self-rising flour

¼ tsp baking powder

4 tbsp unsweetened cocoa

3½ oz/100 g/ ½ cup
    superfine sugar

2 eggs

2 tbsp corn syrup

5 fl oz/150 ml/²/₃ cup corn oil

5 fl oz/150 ml/²/₃ cup milk

filling

1 tsp instant coffee

1 tbsp boiling water

10 fl oz/300 ml/1¼ cups
    heavy cream

2 tbsp confectioners' sugar

to decorate

1¾ oz/50 g semisweet
    chocolate, grated

chocolate caraque

confectioners' sugar,
    for dusting

method

1 Sift the flour, baking powder, and cocoa into a large bowl, then stir in the sugar. Make a well in the center and stir in the eggs, syrup, corn oil, and milk. Beat with a wooden spoon, gradually mixing in the dry ingredients to make a smooth batter. Divide the mixture between 3 lightly greased 3 x 7-inch/18-cm cake pans.

2 Bake in a preheated oven, 350°F/180°C, for 35–45 minutes, or until springy to the touch. Let stand in the pans for 5 minutes, then turn out and let cool completely on a wire rack.

3 To make the filling, dissolve the instant coffee in the boiling water and place in a large bowl with the cream and confectioners' sugar. Whip until the cream is just holding its shape, then use half the cream to sandwich the 3 cakes together. Spread the remaining cream over the top and sides of the cake. Press the grated chocolate into the cream round the edge of the cake.

4 Transfer the cake to a serving plate. Lay the chocolate caraque over the top of the cake. Cut a few thin strips of parchment paper and place on top of the chocolate caraque. Dust lightly with confectioners' sugar, then carefully remove the paper. Serve.

chocolate ganache cake

ingredients

SERVES 10

6 oz/175 g/³/₄ cup butter

6 oz/175 g/³/₄ cup
   superfine sugar

4 eggs, beaten lightly

7 oz/200 g/1³/₄ cups
   self-rising flour

1 tbsp unsweetened cocoa

1³/₄ oz/50 g semisweet
   chocolate, melted

ganache

16 fl oz/450 ml/2 cups
   heavy cream

13 oz/375 g semisweet
   chocolate, broken
   into pieces

7 oz/200 g chocolate-flavored
   cake covering, to finish

method

1 Beat the butter and sugar until light and fluffy. Gradually add the eggs, beating well. Sift the flour and cocoa together. Fold into the cake mixture. Fold in the melted chocolate.

2 Pour into a lightly greased and base-lined 8-inch/20-cm springform cake pan and smooth the top. Bake in a preheated oven, 350°F/180°C, for 40 minutes or until springy to the touch. Let cool for 5 minutes in the pan, then turn out onto a wire rack. Cut the cold cake into 2 layers.

3 To make the ganache, place the cream in a pan and bring to a boil, stirring. Add the chocolate and stir until melted and combined. Pour into a bowl and whisk for about 5 minutes or until fluffy and cool. Set aside one-third of the ganache and use the rest to sandwich the cake together and spread smoothly and evenly over the top and sides of the cake.

4 Melt the cake covering and spread it over a large sheet of baking parchment. Let cool until just set. Cut into strips a little wider than the height of the cake. Place the strips around the edge of the cake, overlapping them slightly.

5 Using a pastry bag fitted with a fine tip, pipe the reserved ganache in tear drops or shells to cover the top of the cake. Let the cake chill for 1 hour in the refrigerator before serving.

chocolate cake with coffee syrup

ingredients

SERVES 12

4 oz/115 g unsalted butter, plus extra for greasing

8 oz/225 g semisweet chocolate, broken into pieces

1 tbsp strong black coffee

4 large eggs

2 egg yolks

4 oz/115 g/generous 1/2 cup golden superfine sugar

2 oz/55 g/generous 1/3 cup all-purpose flour

2 tsp ground cinnamon

1 3/4 oz/50 g/scant 1/2 cup ground almonds

chocolate-covered coffee beans, to decorate

syrup

10 fl oz/300 ml/1 1/4 cups strong black coffee

4 oz/115 g/generous 1/2 cup golden superfine sugar

1 cinnamon stick

method

1 Place the chocolate, butter, and coffee in a heatproof bowl and set over a pan of gently simmering water until melted. Stir to blend, then remove from the heat and let cool slightly.

2 Place the whole eggs, egg yolks, and sugar in a separate bowl and whisk together until thick and pale. Sift the flour and cinnamon over the egg mixture. Add the almonds and the chocolate mixture and fold in carefully. Spoon the cake batter into a greased and base-lined deep 8-inch/20-cm round cake pan. Bake in a preheated oven, 375°F/190°C, for 35 minutes, or until the tip of a knife inserted into the center comes out clean. Let cool slightly before turning out onto a serving plate.

3 Meanwhile, make the syrup. Place the coffee, sugar, and cinnamon stick in a heavy-bottom pan and heat gently, stirring, until the sugar has dissolved. Increase the heat and boil for 5 minutes, or until reduced and thickened slightly. Keep warm. Pierce the surface of the cake with a toothpick, then drizzle over half the coffee syrup. Decorate with chocolate-covered coffee beans and serve, cut into wedges, with the remaining coffee syrup.

white truffle cake

ingredients

SERVES 12

2 eggs

4 tbsp superfine sugar

2 oz/55 g/generous $^1/_3$ cup
   all-purpose flour

1$^3/_4$ oz/50 g white chocolate,
   melted

truffle topping

10 fl oz/300 ml/1$^1/_4$ cups
   heavy cream

12 oz/350 g white chocolate,
   broken into pieces

9 oz/250 g mascarpone
   cheese

to decorate

semisweet, light, or white
   chocolate caraque

unsweetened cocoa,
   for dusting

method

1 Whisk the eggs and superfine sugar in a mixing bowl for 10 minutes or until the mixture is very light and foamy and the whisk leaves a trail that lasts a few seconds when lifted. Sift the flour and fold in with a metal spoon. Fold in the melted white chocolate. Pour into a greased and lined 8-inch/20-cm round springform cake pan and bake in a preheated oven, 350°F/180°C, for 25 minutes or until springy to the touch. Let cool slightly, then transfer to a wire rack until completely cold. Return the cold cake to the pan.

2 To make the topping, place the cream in a pan and bring to a boil, stirring to prevent it sticking to the bottom of the pan. Cool slightly, then add the white chocolate pieces and stir until melted and combined. Remove from the heat and stir until almost cool, then stir in the mascarpone cheese. Pour the mixture on top of the cake and let chill for 2 hours.

3 Remove the cake from the pan and transfer to a plate. Decorate the top of the cake with the caraque. Dust with cocoa powder.

double chocolate gâteau

ingredients

SERVES 10

filling

9 fl oz/250 ml/generous
    1 cup whipping cream
8 oz/225 g white chocolate,
    broken into pieces

sponge

8 oz/225 g butter, softened,
8 oz/225 g/generous 1 cup
    golden superfine sugar
4 eggs, beaten
6 oz/175 g/generous 1 cup
    self-rising flour
2 oz/55 g/$\frac{1}{2}$ cup
    unsweetened cocoa

frosting

12 oz/350 g semisweet
    chocolate, broken
    into pieces
4 oz/115 g butter
3 fl oz/85 ml/$\frac{1}{3}$ cup
    heavy cream

to decorate

chocolate curls, chilled
4 oz/115 g semisweet
    chocolate, broken
    into pieces
2 tsp confectioners' sugar
    and unsweetened cocoa

method

1 To make the filling, heat the cream to almost boiling. Place the white chocolate in a food processor and chop coarsely. With the motor running, pour the cream through the feed tube. Process for 10–15 seconds, or until the mixture is smooth. Transfer to a bowl and let cool. Cover and let chill for 2 hours, or until firm. Whisk until just starting to hold soft peaks.

2 To make the sponge, beat the butter and sugar together until light and fluffy. Gradually beat in the eggs. Sift the flour and cocoa into another bowl, then fold into the batter. Spoon into a greased and base-lined 8-inch/20-cm deep round cake pan, level the surface, and bake in a preheated oven, 350°F/180°C, for 45–50 minutes, or until springy to the touch and the tip of a knife inserted into the center comes out clean. Let stand in the pan for 5 minutes, then let cool on a wire rack.

3 To make the frosting, melt the chocolate. Stir in the butter and cream. Let cool, stirring frequently, until the mixture is a spreading consistency. Slice the cake into 3 layers. Sandwich the layers together with the filling. Cover the cake with frosting and put chocolate curls on top. Mix together the confectioners' sugar and cocoa and sift over the cake.

almond & hazelnut gâteau

ingredients

SERVES 8

butter, for greasing

4 eggs

3^1/$_2$ oz/100 g/^{1}/$_2$ cup
superfine sugar

1^3/$_4$ oz/50 g/^{1}/$_2$ cup
ground almonds

1^3/$_4$ oz/50 g/^{1}/$_2$ cup
ground hazelnuts

5^1/$_2$ tbsp all-purpose flour

1^3/$_4$ oz/50 g/scant ^{1}/$_2$ cup
slivered almonds

confectioners' sugar,
for dusting

filling

3^1/$_2$ oz/100 g semisweet
chocolate

1 tbsp butter

10 fl oz/300 ml/1^1/$_4$ cups
heavy cream

method

1 Whisk the eggs and superfine sugar together for 10 minutes, or until light and foamy and the whisk leaves a trail that lasts a few seconds when lifted. Fold in the ground almonds and hazelnuts, sift the flour and fold in with a metal spoon or spatula. Pour into 2 lightly greased and base-lined 7-inch/18-cm round sandwich cake pans.

2 Sprinkle the slivered almonds over the top of one of the cakes, then bake both cakes in a preheated oven, 375°F/190°C, for 15–20 minutes, or until springy to the touch. Let cool in the pans for 5 minutes, then turn out onto wire racks to cool completely.

3 To make the filling, melt the chocolate, remove from the heat, and stir in the butter. Let cool. Whip the cream until holding its shape, then fold in the chocolate until mixed.

4 Place the cake without the extra almonds on a serving plate and spread the filling over it. Let set slightly, then place the almond-topped cake on top of the filling and let chill in the refrigerator for 1 hour. Dust with confectioners' sugar and serve.

double chocolate roulade

ingredients

SERVES 8

4 eggs, separated

4 oz/115 g/generous $\frac{1}{2}$ cup
golden superfine sugar

4 oz/115 g semisweet
chocolate, melted
and cooled

1 tsp instant coffee granules,
dissolved in 2 tbsp hot
water, cooled

confectioners' sugar,
to decorate

unsweetened cocoa,
for dusting

fresh raspberries, to serve

filling

9 fl oz/250 ml/generous 1 cup
whipping cream

5 oz/140 g white chocolate,
broken into pieces

3 tbsp Tia Maria

method

1 Line a 9 x 13-inch/23 x 33-cm jelly roll pan with nonstick parchment paper. Whisk the egg yolks and sugar in a bowl until pale and mousse-like. Fold in the chocolate, then the coffee. Place the egg whites in a clean bowl and whisk until stiff but not dry. Stir a little of the egg whites into the chocolate mixture, then fold in the remainder. Pour into the pan and bake in a preheated oven, 350°F/180°C, for 15–20 minutes, or until firm. Cover with a damp dish towel and let stand in the pan for 8 hours, or overnight.

2 Meanwhile, make the filling. Heat the cream until almost boiling. Place the chocolate in a food processor and chop coarsely. With the motor running, pour the cream through the feed tube. Process until smooth. Stir in the Tia Maria. Transfer to a bowl and let cool. Let chill for 8 hours, or overnight.

3 To assemble the roulade, whip the chocolate cream until soft peaks form. Cut a sheet of waxed paper larger than the roulade, place on a counter and sift confectioners' sugar over it. Turn the roulade out onto the paper. Peel away the lining paper. Spread the chocolate cream over the roulade and roll up from the short side nearest to you. Transfer to a dish, seam-side down. Let chill for 2 hours, then dust with cocoa. Serve with raspberries.

chocolate passion cake

ingredients

SERVES 6

butter, for greasing

5 eggs

5^1/$_2$ oz/150 g/generous
^{3}/$_4$ cup superfine sugar

5^1/$_2$ oz/150 g/1 cup
all-purpose flour

1^1/$_2$ oz/40 g/generous ^{3}/$_8$ cup
unsweetened cocoa

6 oz/175 g carrots, peeled,
finely grated, and
squeezed until dry

1^3/$_4$ oz/50 g/generous ^{3}/$_8$ cup
chopped walnuts

2 tbsp corn oil

12 oz/350 g/1^1/$_2$ cups
medium-fat soft cheese

6 oz/175 g/1^1/$_2$ cups
confectioners' sugar

6 oz/175 g milk or semisweet
chocolate, melted

method

1 Place the eggs and sugar in a large bowl set over a pan of gently simmering water and, using an electric whisk, whisk until the mixture is very thick and the whisk leaves a trail that lasts a few seconds when lifted.

2 Remove the bowl from the heat. Sift the flour and cocoa into the bowl and carefully fold in. Fold in the carrots, walnuts, and corn oil until the cake batter is just blended.

3 Pour into a lightly greased and base-lined 8-inch/20-cm deep round cake pan and bake in a preheated oven, 375°F/190°C, for 45 minutes. Let cool slightly, then turn out onto a wire rack to cool completely.

4 Beat the soft cheese and confectioners' sugar together until blended, then beat in the melted chocolate. Split the cake in half and sandwich together again with half the chocolate mixture. Cover the top of the cake with the remainder of the chocolate mixture, swirling it with a knife. Let chill in the refrigerator or serve immediately.

chocolate & orange cake

ingredients

SERVES 8

6 oz/175 g/³/4 cup superfine
   sugar
6 oz/175 g/³/4 cup butter or
   block margarine
3 eggs, beaten
6 oz/175 g/1¹/2 cups self-
   rising flour, sifted
2 tbsp unsweetened cocoa,
   sifted
2 tbsp milk
3 tbsp orange juice
grated rind of ¹/2 orange

frosting

6 oz/175 g/1¹/2 cups
   confectioners' sugar
2 tbsp orange juice
a little melted chocolate

method

1 Beat the sugar and butter or margarine together in a bowl until light and fluffy. Gradually add the eggs, beating well after each addition. Carefully fold in the flour.

2 Divide the mixture in half. Add the cocoa and milk to one half, stirring until well combined. Flavor the other half with the orange juice and grated orange rind.

3 Place spoonfuls of each mixture into a lightly greased 8-inch/20-cm deep round cake pan and swirl together with a skewer, to create a marbled effect. Bake in a preheated oven, 375°F/190°C, for 25 minutes or until the cake is springy to the touch. Let cool in the pan for a few minutes before transferring to a wire rack to cool completely.

4 To make the frosting, sift the confectioner's sugar into a mixing bowl and mix in enough of the orange juice to form a smooth frosting. Spread the frosting over the top of the cake and leave to set. Pipe fine lines of melted chocolate in a decorated pattern over the top.

date & chocolate cake

ingredients

SERVES 6

4 oz/115 g semisweet
  chocolate
1 tbsp grenadine
1 tbsp corn syrup
4 oz/115 g unsalted butter
  plus extra for greasing
2 oz/55 g/generous ¼ cup
  superfine sugar
2 large eggs
3 oz/85 g/½ cup self-rising
  flour plus extra for dusting
2 tbsp ground rice
1 tbsp confectioners' sugar,
  to decorate

filling

4 oz/115 g/⅔ cup dried
  dates, chopped
1 tbsp orange juice
1 tbsp raw sugar
1 oz/25 g/⅛ cup blanched
  almonds, chopped
2 tbsp apricot jelly

method

1 Break the chocolate into pieces, then place the chocolate, grenadine, and syrup in the top of a double boiler or in a heatproof bowl set over a pan of barely simmering water. Stir over low heat until the chocolate has melted and the mixture is smooth. Remove the pan from the heat and let cool.

2 Beat the butter and superfine sugar together in a bowl until pale and fluffy. Gradually beat in the eggs, then beat in the chocolate mixture. Sift the flour into another bowl and stir in the ground rice. Fold the 2 mixtures together.

3 Divide the cake batter between 2 greased 7-inch/18-cm sandwich cake pans, dusted with flour, and level the surface. Bake in a preheated oven, 350°F/180°C, for 20–25 minutes, or until golden and firm to the touch. Turn out onto a wire rack to cool.

4 To make the filling, put all the ingredients into a pan and stir over low heat for 4–5 minutes, or until fully blended. Remove from the heat, let cool, then use the filling to sandwich the cakes together. Dust the top of the cake with confectioners' sugar and serve.

chocolate marshmallow cake

ingredients

SERVES 6

6 tbsp unsalted butter

8 oz/225 g/generous 1 cup
   superfine sugar

$1/2$ tsp vanilla extract

2 eggs, beaten lightly

3 oz/85 g semisweet chocolate,
   broken into pieces

5 fl oz/150 ml/$2/3$ cup
   buttermilk

6 oz/175 g/$1^1/4$ cups
   self-rising flour

$1/2$ tsp baking soda

pinch of salt

frosting

6 oz/175 g white
   marshmallows

1 tbsp milk

2 egg whites

2 tbsp superfine sugar

2 oz/55 g light chocolate,
   grated, to decorate

method

1 Cream the butter, sugar, and vanilla together in a bowl until pale and fluffy, then gradually beat in the eggs.

2 Melt the chocolate in a bowl over a pan of simmering water. Stir in the buttermilk gradually until well combined. Let cool slightly.

3 Sift the flour, baking soda, and salt into a separate bowl. Add the chocolate and the flour mixtures alternately to the creamed mixture, a little at a time. Spoon the mixture into a greased $1^1/2$-pint/850-ml/$3^1/3$-cup ovenproof bowl greased with butter and smooth the surface. Bake in a preheated oven, 325°F/ 160°C, for 50 minutes until a skewer inserted into the center of the cake comes out clean. Turn out onto a wire rack to cool.

4 Meanwhile, make the frosting. Heat the marshmallows and milk very gently in a small pan until the marshmallows have melted. Remove from the heat and let cool. Whisk the egg whites until soft peaks form, then add the sugar and continue whisking, until stiff peaks form. Fold into the cooled marshmallow mixture and set aside for 10 minutes.

5 When the cake is cool, cover the top and sides with the marshmallow frosting. Top with grated light chocolate.

family chocolate cake

ingredients

SERVES 8

$4^1/_2$ oz/125 g/$^1/_2$ cup soft
  margarine

$4^1/_2$ oz/125 g/$^1/_2$ cup
  superfine sugar

2 eggs

1 tbsp light corn syrup

$4^1/_2$ oz/125 g/1 cup self-rising
  flour, sifted

2 tbsp unsweetened cocoa,
  sifted

filling and topping

4 tbsp confectioners' sugar,
  sifted

2 tbsp butter

$3^1/_2$ oz/100 g white or light
  cooking chocolate

a little light or white chocolate,
  melted (optional)

method

1 Place all of the ingredients for the cake in a large mixing bowl and beat with a wooden spoon or electric mixer to form a smooth mixture.

2 Divide the mixture between 2 lightly greased 7-inch/18-cm shallow cake pans and smooth the tops. Bake in a preheated oven, 375°F/ 190°C, for 20 minutes or until springy to the touch. Cool for a few minutes in the pans then transfer to a wire rack to cool completely.

3 To make the filling, beat the sugar and butter together in a bowl until light and fluffy. Melt the white or light cooking chocolate and beat half into the icing mixture. Use the filling to sandwich the 2 cakes together.

4 Spread the remaining melted cooking chocolate over the top of the cake. Pipe circles of contrasting light or white chocolate and feather into the cooking chocolate with a toothpick, if desired. Let the cake set before serving.

mocha cupcakes with whipped cream

ingredients

MAKES 20 CUPCAKES

2 tbsp instant espresso coffee powder

6 tbsp butter

3^1/$_2$ oz/100 g/generous ^{3}/$_8$ cup superfine sugar

1 tbsp honey

8 fl oz/250 ml/scant 1 cup water

8 oz/225 g/scant 1^5/$_8$ cups all-purpose flour

2 tbsp unsweetened cocoa

1 tsp baking soda

3 tbsp milk

1 large egg, lightly beaten

topping

8 fl oz/225 ml/1 cup whipping cream

unsweetened cocoa, sifted, for dusting

method

1 Put 20 paper baking cases in 2 muffin pans, or put 20 double-layer paper cases on 2 cookie sheets.

2 Put the coffee powder, butter, sugar, honey, and water in a pan and heat gently, stirring, until the sugar has dissolved. Bring to a boil, then reduce the heat and let simmer for 5 minutes. Pour into a large heatproof bowl and let cool.

3 When the mixture has cooled, sift in the flour and cocoa. Dissolve the baking soda in the milk, then add to the mixture with the egg and beat together until smooth. Spoon the batter into the paper cases.

4 Bake the cupcakes in a preheated oven, 350°F/180°C, for 15–20 minutes, or until well risen and firm to the touch. Transfer to a wire rack to cool.

5 For the topping, whisk the cream in a bowl until it holds its shape. Just before serving, spoon heaping teaspoonfuls of cream on top of each cake, then dust lightly with sifted cocoa. Store the cupcakes in the refrigerator until ready to serve.

chocolate butterfly cakes

ingredients

MAKES 12 CUPCAKES

8 tbsp soft margarine

$3^1/_2$ oz/100 g/$^1/_2$ cup
   superfine sugar

8 oz/225 g/scant $1^5/_8$ cups
   self-rising white flour

2 large eggs

2 tbsp unsweetened cocoa

1 oz/25 g semisweet
   chocolate, melted

confectioners' sugar,
   for dusting

filling

6 tbsp butter, softened

6 oz/165 g/$1^1/_2$ cups
   confectioners' sugar

1 oz/25 g semisweet
   chocolate, melted

method

1 Put 12 paper baking cases in a muffin pan, or put 12 double-layer paper cases on a cookie sheet.

2 Put the margarine, sugar, flour, eggs, and cocoa in a large bowl and, using an electric hand whisk, beat together until just smooth. Beat in the melted chocolate. Spoon the batter into the paper cases.

3 Bake the cupcakes in a preheated oven, 350°F/180°C, for 15 minutes, or until springy to the touch. Transfer to a wire rack and let cool.

4 To make the filling, put the butter in a bowl and beat until fluffy. Sift in the confectioners' sugar and beat together until smooth. Add the melted chocolate and beat together until well mixed.

5 When the cupcakes are cold, use a serrated knife to cut a circle from the top of each cake and then cut each circle in half. Spread or pipe a little of the buttercream into the center of each cupcake and press the 2 semicircular halves into it at an angle to resemble butterfly wings. Dust with sifted confectioners' sugar before serving.

warm molten-centered chocolate cupcakes

ingredients

MAKES 8 CUPS

4 tbsp soft margarine

2 oz/55 g/generous $^1/_4$ cup
  superfine sugar

1 large egg

3 oz/85 g/scant $^5/_8$ cup
  self-rising flour

1 tbsp unsweetened cocoa

2 oz/55 g semisweet chocolate

confectioners' sugar,
  for dusting

method

1 Put 8 paper baking cases in a muffin pan, or place 8 double-layer paper cases on a cookie sheet.

2 Put the margarine, sugar, egg, flour, and cocoa in a large bowl and, using an electric hand whisk, beat together until just smooth.

3 Spoon half of the batter into the paper cases. Using a teaspoon, make an indentation in the center of each cake. Break the chocolate evenly into 8 squares and place a piece in each indentation, then spoon the remaining cake batter on top.

4 Bake the cupcakes in a preheated oven, 375°F/190°C, for 20 minutes, or until well risen and springy to the touch. Let stand for 2–3 minutes before serving warm, dusted with sifted confectioners' sugar.

dark & white chocolate torte

ingredients

SERVES 6

butter, for greasing

4 eggs

3^1/$_2$ oz/100 g/^{1}/$_2$ cup
   superfine sugar

3^1/$_2$ oz//100 g/^{3}/$_4$ cup
   all-purpose flour

filling

10 fl oz/300 ml/1^1/$_4$ cups
   heavy cream

5^1/$_2$ oz/150 g semisweet
   chocolate, broken into
   small pieces

topping

2^3/$_4$ oz/75 g white chocolate

1 tbsp butter

1 tbsp milk

4 tbsp confectioners' sugar

shavings of chocolate, to
   decorate

method

1 Whisk the eggs and superfine sugar in a large bowl with an electric whisk for 10 minutes, or until the mixture is very light and foamy and the whisk leaves a trail that lasts a few seconds when lifted.

2 Sift the flour and fold in with a metal spoon or spatula. Pour into a greased and base-lined 8-inch/20-cm round springform cake pan and bake in a preheated oven, 350°F/180°C, for 35–40 minutes, or until springy to the touch. Let cool slightly, then transfer to a wire rack to cool completely.

3 For the filling, place the cream in a pan and bring to a boil, stirring. Add the chocolate and stir until melted. Remove from the heat, transfer to a bowl, and let cool. Beat with a wooden spoon until thick.

4 Slice the cold cake horizontally into 2 layers. Sandwich the layers together with the semisweet chocolate cream and place on a wire rack.

5 For the topping, melt the chocolate and butter together and stir until blended. Whisk in the milk and confectioners' sugar. Continue whisking for a few minutes until the frosting is cool. Pour it over the cake and spread with a spatula to coat the top and sides. Let set.

chocolate brandy torte

ingredients

SERVES 12

base

3¹/2 oz/100 g butter, plus extra
  for greasing
9 oz/250 g gingersnaps
2³/4 oz/75 g semisweet
  chocolate

filling

8 oz/225 g semisweet chocolate
9 oz/250 g/generous 1 cup
  mascarpone cheese
2 eggs, separated
3 tbsp brandy
10 fl oz/300 ml/1¹/4 cups
  heavy cream
4 tbsp superfine sugar

to decorate

3¹/2 fl oz/100 ml/generous
  ¹/3 cup heavy cream
chocolate-covered coffee beans

method

1 Place the gingersnaps in a plastic bag and crush with a rolling pin. Transfer to a bowl. Place the chocolate and butter in a small pan and heat gently until melted, then pour over the cookies. Mix well, then press into a greased 9-inch/23-cm springform cake pan. Let chill while preparing the filling.

2 To make the filling, place the chocolate in a heatproof bowl and set over a pan of simmering water, stirring, until melted. Remove from the heat and beat in the mascarpone cheese, egg yolks, and brandy. Whip the cream until just holding its shape. Fold in the chocolate mixture.

3 Whisk the egg whites in a spotlessly clean, greasefree bowl until soft peaks form. Add the sugar, a little at a time, and whisk until thick and glossy. Fold into the chocolate mixture, in 2 batches, until just mixed.

4 Spoon the mixture into the prepared base and let chill in the refrigerator for at least 2 hours. Carefully transfer to a serving plate. To decorate, whip the cream and pipe onto the cheesecake, add the chocolate-covered coffee beans, and serve.

chocolate & almond torte

ingredients

SERVES 10

8 oz/225 g semisweet
chocolate, broken
into pieces

3 tbsp water

5^1/$_2$ oz/150 g/1 cup
brown sugar

6 oz/175 g/^{3}/$_4$ cup butter,
softened, plus extra
for greasing

1oz/25 g/^{1}/$_4$ cup ground
almonds

3 tbsp self-rising flour

5 eggs, separated

3^1/$_2$ oz/100 g/^{2}/$_3$ cup finely
chopped blanched
almonds

confectioners' sugar,
for dusting

fresh berries and heavy
cream, to serve

method

1 Melt the chocolate with the water in a pan set over very low heat, stirring until smooth. Add the sugar and stir until dissolved, taking the pan off the heat to prevent it overheating.

2 Add the butter in small amounts until it has melted into the chocolate. Remove from the heat and lightly stir in the ground almonds and flour. Add the egg yolks one at a time, beating well after each addition.

3 Whisk the egg whites in a large mixing bowl, until they stand in soft peaks, then fold them into the chocolate mixture with a metal spoon. Stir in the chopped almonds. Pour the mixture into a greased and base-lined 9-inch/23-cm loose-bottom cake pan and smooth the surface.

4 Bake in a preheated oven, 350°F/180°C, for 40–45 minutes, until well risen and firm (the cake will crack on the surface during cooking).

5 Let cool in the pan for 30–40 minutes, then turn out onto a wire rack to cool completely. Dust with confectioners' sugar and serve in slices with fresh berries and cream.

chocolate truffle torte

ingredients

SERVES 10

butter, for greasing

2 oz/55 g/generous $1/4$ cup
golden superfine sugar

2 eggs

1 oz/25 g/scant $1/4$ cup
all-purpose flour

1 oz/25 g/$1/4$ cup
unsweetened cocoa, plus
extra to decorate

2 fl oz/50 ml/$1/4$ cup cold
strong black coffee

2 tbsp brandy

topping

1 pint/600 ml/$2^1/2$ cups
whipping cream

15 oz/425 g semisweet
chocolate, melted and
cooled

confectioners' sugar,
to decorate

method

1 Place the sugar and eggs in a heatproof bowl and set over a pan of hot water. Whisk together until pale and mousse-like. Sift the flour and unsweetened cocoa into a separate bowl, then fold gently into the cake batter. Pour into a greased and base-lined 9-inch/23-cm springform cake pan and bake in a preheated oven, 425°F/220°C, for 7–10 minutes, or until risen and firm to the touch.

2 Transfer to a wire rack to cool. Wash and dry the pan and replace the cooled cake in the pan. Mix the coffee and brandy together and brush over the cake.

3 To make the topping, place the cream in a bowl and whip until very soft peaks form. Carefully fold in the cooled chocolate. Pour the mixture over the sponge. Let chill in the refrigerator for 4–5 hours, or until set.

4 To decorate the torte, sift unsweetened cocoa over the top and remove carefully from the pan. Using strips of card or waxed paper, sift bands of confectioners' sugar over the torte to create a striped pattern. To serve, cut into slices with a hot knife.

cookies,
bars & bakes

This chapter seems to hold the solution to every problem—what to put in the children's lunch bags, what to give them when they come home from school, what to offer as a gift to an aged aunt who has everything, what to make for the bake sale, what to serve the friends who are coming for morning coffee or afternoon tea, even what to do on a rainy day.

Home-made cookies, bars, and bakes are so much more special than bought ones, and you really can whip up a batch of your favorite recipe in almost no time. For a treat in a lunch bag, go for something that includes a hint of fruit as well as chocolate, such as apricot and chocolate chip cookies or chocolate and apple oaties. To give as a gift, why not try nutty chocolate drizzles, chocolate temptations, or, at Christmas, lebkuchen, those delicious soft, spicy cookies with an evocative aroma of the festive season. Cappuccino squares or mocha brownies are the natural partner with morning coffee, and chocolate chip shortbread with afternoon tea. Brownies never fail at a bake sale, and checkerboard cookies are eye-catching, too.

And for that rainy day—well, what about caramel chocolate shortbread? It'll really cheer you up!

nutty chocolate drizzles

ingredients

MAKES 24 COOKIES

8 oz/250 g/1 cup butter or margarine, plus extra for greasing

$11^1/_2$ oz/325 g/$1^1/_2$ cups raw brown sugar

1 egg

5 oz/140 g/1 cup all-purpose flour, sifted

1 tsp baking powder

1 tsp baking soda

5 oz/140 g/$1^1/_2$ cups rolled oats

1 oz/30 g/$^1/_4$ cup bran

1 oz/30 g/$^1/_4$ cup wheatgerm

3 oz/85 g/$^3/_4$ cup mixed nuts, toasted and chopped coarsely

6 oz/175 g/scant $1^1/_4$ cups semisweet chocolate chips

4 oz/55 g/$^2/_3$ cup raisins and golden raisins

6 oz/175 g semisweet chocolate, chopped coarsely

method

1 In a large bowl, cream together the butter, sugar, and egg. Add the flour, baking powder, baking soda, oats, bran, and wheatgerm and mix together until well combined. Stir in the nuts, chocoate chips, and dried fruit.

2 Put 24 rounded tablespoonfuls of the cookie mixture onto a large greased cookie sheet. Transfer to a preheated oven, 350°F/180°C, and bake for 12 minutes, or until the cookies are golden brown.

3 Remove the cookies from the oven, then transfer to a wire rack and let cool. While they are cooling, put the chocolate pieces into a heatproof bowl over a pan of gently simmering water and heat until melted. Stir the chocolate, then let cool slightly. Use a spoon to drizzle the chocolate in waves over the cookies, or spoon it into a piping nozzle and pipe zigzag lines over the cookies. Store in an airtight container in the refrigerator before serving.

white chocolate cookies

ingredients

MAKES 24

$4^{1}/_{2}$ oz/125 g butter, softened, plus extra for greasing

$4^{1}/_{2}$ oz/125 g/$^{5}/_{8}$ cup firmly packed soft brown sugar

1 egg, beaten

7 oz/200 g/generous $1^{1}/_{4}$ cups self-rising flour

pinch of salt

$4^{1}/_{2}$ oz/125 g white chocolate, coarsely chopped

$1^{3}/_{4}$ oz/50 g/generous $^{1}/_{4}$ cup Brazil nuts, chopped

method

1 Lightly grease several cookie sheets, enough to accommodate 24 cookies. Beat the butter and sugar together in a large bowl until light and fluffy. Gradually add the beaten egg to the cookie batter, beating well after each addition.

2 Sift the flour and salt into the cookie batter and blend well. Stir in the white chocolate chunks and the chopped Brazil nuts.

3 Drop heaped teaspoons of the batter onto the cookie sheets. Do not put more than 6 teaspoons of the batter onto each sheet as they will spread during cooking.

4 Bake in a preheated oven, 375°F/190°C, for 10–12 minutes, or until just golden brown. Transfer the cookies to wire racks and let stand until completely cold before serving.

chocolate butter cookies

ingredients

SERVES 4

3¹/₂ oz/100 g butter, softened,
    plus extra for greasing
3¹/₂ oz/100 g/¹/₂ cup
    superfine sugar
1 egg yolk
8 oz/225 g/1¹/₂ cups
    all-purpose flour, sifted,
    plus extra for dusting
about 2 tbsp milk

frosting

9 oz/250 g/scant 1¹/₂ cups
    confectioners' sugar, sifted
1 tbsp unsweetened cocoa
    powder
about 3 tbsp orange juice

method

1 Put the butter and all but a tablespoon of the sugar into a large bowl and cream until pale and fluffy. Beat in the egg yolk, then add the flour and mix well. Stir in enough milk to form a smooth dough.

2 Roll out the dough on a lightly floured work surface. Cut out rounds using a 3-inch/7.5-cm cookie cutter. Arrange the circles on 2 large, greased cookie sheets, leaving enough space between them to allow them to spread during cooking. Sprinkle over the remaining sugar and bake in a preheated oven, 400°F/200°C, for 15 minutes, or until golden. Remove the cookies from the oven, transfer to wire racks, and let cool completely.

3 To make the frosting, put the confectioners' sugar and cocoa powder into a bowl. Stir in the orange juice gradually until enough has been added to make a thin frosting. Put a teaspoonful of frosting on each cookie and let set before serving.

double chocolate chip cookies

ingredients

MAKES ABOUT 24

7 oz/200 g butter, softened,
    plus extra for greasing
7 oz/200 g/1 cup golden
    superfine sugar
$^1/_2$ tsp vanilla extract
1 large egg
8 oz/225 g/generous $1^1/_2$ cups
    all-purpose flour
pinch of salt
1 tsp baking soda
4 oz/115 g/$^2/_3$ cup white
    chocolate chips
4 oz/115 g/$^2/_3$ cup semisweet
    chocolate chips

method

1 Place the butter, sugar, and vanilla extract in a large bowl and beat together. Gradually beat in the egg until the cookie batter is light and fluffy.

2 Sift the flour, salt, and baking soda over the cookie batter and fold in, then fold in the chocolate chips.

3 Drop dessertspoonfuls of the cookie batter onto 2 greased cookie sheets, allowing room for expansion during cooking. Bake in a preheated oven, 350°F/180°C, for 10–12 minutes, or until crisp outside but still soft inside. Let cool on the cookie sheets for 2 minutes, then transfer to wire racks to cool completely.

chocolate chip oaties

ingredients

MAKES ABOUT 20

4 oz/115 g butter, softened,
plus extra for greasing

4 oz/115 g/^{1}/$_2$ cup firmly
packed light brown sugar

1 egg

3^1/$_2$ oz/100 g/1 cup
rolled oats

1 tbsp milk

1 tsp vanilla extract

4^1/$_2$ oz/125 g/scant 1 cup
all-purpose flour

1 tbsp unsweetened cocoa

^{1}/$_2$ tsp baking powder

6 oz/175 g semisweet
chocolate, broken
into pieces

6 oz/175 g milk chocolate,
broken into pieces

method

1 Place the butter and sugar in a bowl and beat together until light and fluffy. Beat in the egg, then add the oats, milk, and vanilla extract. Beat together until well blended. Sift the flour, unsweetened cocoa, and baking powder into the cookie batter and stir. Stir in the chocolate pieces.

2 Place dessertspoonfuls of the cookie batter on 2 greased cookie sheets and flatten slightly with a fork. Bake in a preheated oven, 350°F/180°C, for 15 minutes, or until slightly risen and firm. Let cool on the cookie sheets for 2 minutes, then transfer to wire racks to cool completely.

mocha walnut cookies

ingredients

MAKES ABOUT 16

4 oz/115 g butter, softened,
    plus extra for greasing
4 oz/115 g/^{1}/$_2$ cup firmly
    packed light brown sugar
3 oz/85 g/^{3}/$_8$ cup golden
    granulated sugar
1 tsp vanilla extract
1 tbsp instant coffee
    granules, dissolved in
    1 tbsp hot water
1 egg
6oz/175 g/1 cup
    all-purpose flour
^{1}/$_2$ tsp baking powder
^{1}/$_4$ tsp baking soda
2 oz/55 g/^{1}/$_3$ cup milk
    chocolate chips
2 oz/55 g/^{1}/$_4$ cup shelled
    walnuts, coarsely chopped

method

1 Place the butter, brown sugar, and granulated sugar in a large mixing bowl and beat together thoroughly until light and fluffy. Place the vanilla extract, coffee, and egg in a separate bowl and whisk together.

2 Gradually add the coffee mixture to the butter and sugar, beating until fluffy. Sift the flour, baking powder, and baking soda into the cookie batter and fold in carefully. Fold in the chocolate chips and walnuts.

3 Place dessertspoonfuls of the cookie batter onto 2 greased cookie sheets, allowing room for the cookies to spread. Bake in a preheated oven, 350°F/180°C, for 10–15 minutes, or until crisp on the outside but still soft inside. Let cool on the cookie sheets for 2 minutes, then transfer to wire racks and let cool completely.

apricot & chocolate chip cookies

ingredients

MAKES 12–14

3 oz/85 g butter, softened, plus extra for greasing

2 tbsp golden granulated sugar

2 oz/55 g/$^1/_4$ cup light brown sugar

$^1/_2$ tsp vanilla extract

1 egg, beaten

6 oz/175 g/generous 1 cup self-rising flour

4 oz/115 g semisweet chocolate, coarsely chopped

4 oz/115 g/$^2/_3$ cup no-soak dried apricots, coarsely chopped

method

1 Place the butter, granulated sugar, brown sugar, and vanilla extract in a bowl and beat together. Gradually beat in the egg until light and fluffy.

2 Sift the flour over the cookie batter and fold in, then fold in the chocolate and apricots.

3 Put tablespoonfuls of the cookie batter onto 2 greased cookie sheets, allowing space for the cookies to spread. Bake in a preheated oven, 350°F/180°C, for 13–15 minutes, or until crisp outside but still soft inside. Let cool on the cookie sheets for 2 minutes, then transfer to wire racks to cool completely.

chocolate & apple oaties

ingredients

MAKES 24 COOKIES

4 oz/115 g/^{1}/$_2$ cup butter or
   margarine, plus extra
   for greasing

4 oz/115 g/^{2}/$_3$ cup apple
   sauce

2 tbsp apple juice

3^1/$_2$ oz/300 g/^{1}/$_2$ cup raw
   brown sugar

1 tsp baking soda

1 tsp almond extract

2 fl oz/50 ml/^{1}/$_4$ cup
   boiling water

4^1/$_2$ oz/125 g/1^1/$_3$ cups
   rolled oats

10 oz/280 g/2 cups all-
   purpose flour, unsifted

pinch of salt

2 oz/55 g/^{1}/$_3$ cup semisweet
   chocolate chips

method

1 Blend the apple sauce, apple juice, butter (or margarine), and sugar in a food processor until a fluffy consistency is reached.

2 In a separate bowl, mix together the baking soda, almond extract, and water, then add to the food processor and mix with the apple mixture. In another bowl, mix together the oats, flour, and salt, then gradually stir into the apple mixture and beat well. Stir in the chocolate chips.

3 Put 24 rounded tablespoonfuls of mixture onto a large cookie sheet, ensuring that they are well spaced. Transfer to a preheated oven, 400°F/200°C, and bake for 15 minutes, or until the cookies are golden brown.

4 Remove the cookies from the oven, then transfer to a wire rack and let them cool completely before serving.

chocolate orange cookies

ingredients

MAKES 30

6 tbsp butter, softened

6 tbsp superfine sugar

1 egg

1 tbsp milk

8 oz/225 g/1^1/$_2$ cups all-
purpose flour, plus extra
for dusting

2 tbsp unsweetened cocoa

frosting

6 oz/175 g/1^1/$_2$ cups
confectioners' sugar, sifted

3 tbsp orange juice

1 oz/25 g semisweet
chocolate, melted

method

1 Beat the butter and sugar together until light and fluffy. Beat in the egg and milk until well blended. Sift the flour and cocoa together and gradually mix together to form a soft dough. Use your fingers to incorporate the last of the flour and bring the dough together.

2 Roll out the dough on a lightly floured counter until ^{1}/$_4$-inch/5-mm thick. Using a 2-inch/5-cm fluted round cutter, cut out as many cookies as you can. Re-roll the dough trimmings and cut out more cookies. Place the cookies on 2 cookie sheets lined with sheets of parchment paper, allowing room for expansion during cooking, and bake in a preheated oven, 350°F/180°C, for 10–12 minutes, or until golden brown.

3 Let the cookies cool on the cookie sheet for a few minutes, then transfer to a wire rack and let cool completely.

4 To make the frosting, place the sugar in a bowl and stir in enough orange juice to form a thin frosting that will coat the back of a spoon. Spread the frosting over the cookies and let set. Drizzle with melted chocolate. Let set before serving.

chocolate temptations

ingredients

MAKES 24 COOKIES

12$\frac{1}{2}$ oz/365 g semisweet
    chocolate
6 tbsp unsalted butter, plus
    extra for greasing
1 tsp strong coffee
2 eggs
5 oz/150 g/scant $\frac{3}{4}$ cup soft
    brown sugar
8 oz/225 g/generous 1$\frac{1}{3}$
    cups all-purpose flour
$\frac{1}{4}$ tsp baking powder
pinch of salt
2 tsp almond extract
1$\frac{3}{4}$ oz/50 g/scant $\frac{2}{3}$ cup
    Brazil nuts, chopped
1$\frac{3}{4}$ oz/50 g/scant $\frac{2}{3}$ cup
    hazelnuts, chopped
1$\frac{1}{2}$ oz/40 g white chocolate

method

1 Put 8 oz/225 g of the semisweet chocolate with the butter and coffee into a heatproof bowl over a pan of simmering water and heat until the chocolate is almost melted.

2 Meanwhile, beat the eggs in a bowl until fluffy. Whisk in the sugar gradually until thick. Remove the chocolate from the heat and stir until smooth. Stir it into the egg mixture until combined.

3 Sift the flour, baking powder, and salt into a bowl and stir into the chocolate mixture. Chop 3 oz/85 g of semisweet chocolate into pieces and stir into the dough. Stir in the almond extract and nuts.

4 Put 24 rounded dessertspoonfuls of the dough on a greased cookie sheet and bake in a preheated oven, 350°F/180°C, for 16 minutes. Transfer the cookies to a wire rack to cool. To decorate, melt the remaining chocolate (semisweet and white) in turn, then spoon into a piping bag and pipe lines onto the cookies.

chocolate viennese fingers

ingredients

MAKES ABOUT 30

4 oz/115 g butter, softened,
   plus extra for greasing
2 oz/55 g/$^1/_2$ cup golden
   confectioners' sugar, sifted
4$^1/_2$ oz/125 g/generous
   $^3/_4$ cup all-purpose flour
1 tbsp unsweetened cocoa
3$^1/_2$ oz/100 g semisweet
   chocolate, melted
   and cooled

method

1 Beat the butter and sugar together until light and fluffy. Sift the flour and unsweetened cocoa into the bowl and work the mixture until it is a smooth, piping consistency.

2 Spoon into a large pastry bag fitted with a 1-inch/2.5-cm fluted tip. Pipe 2$^1/_2$-inch/6-cm lengths of the mixture onto 2 greased cookie sheets, allowing room for expansion during cooking. Bake in a preheated oven, 350°F/180°C, for 15 minutes, or until firm.

3 Let cool on the cookie sheets for 2 minutes, then transfer to a wire rack to cool completely. Dip the ends of the cookies into the melted chocolate and let set before serving.

dutch macaroons

ingredients

MAKES 20

2 egg whites

8 oz/225 g/generous 1 cup
   superfine sugar

6 oz/175 g/generous $1^5/8$
   cups ground almonds

8 oz/225 g semisweet
   chocolate

rice paper

method

1 Whisk the egg whites in a large, clean bowl until stiff, then fold in the sugar and ground almonds.

2 Place the mixture in a large pastry bag fitted with a $1/2$-inch/1-cm plain tip and pipe fingers, 3-inches/7.5-cm long, onto 2 cookie sheets lined with rice paper, allowing room for expansion during cooking.

3 Bake in a preheated oven, 350°F/180°C, for 15–20 minutes, or until golden. Transfer to a wire rack and let cool. Remove the excess rice paper from round the edges.

4 Melt the chocolate and dip the base of each cookie into the chocolate. Place the macaroons on a sheet of parchment paper and let set. Drizzle any remaining chocolate over the top of the cookies (you may have to reheat the chocolate to do this). Let set before serving.

lebkuchen

ingredients

MAKES ABOUT 60

3 eggs

7 oz/200 g/1 cup golden
   superfine sugar

2 oz/55 g/scant $^1/_2$ cup all-
   purpose flour

2 tsp unsweetened cocoa

1 tsp ground cinnamon

$^1/_2$ tsp ground cardamom

$^1/_4$ tsp ground cloves

$^1/_4$ tsp ground nutmeg

6 oz/175 g/1$^1/_2$ cups
   ground almonds

2 oz/55 g/$^1/_3$ cup candied
   peel, finely chopped

to decorate

4 oz/115 g semisweet
   chocolate, melted
   and cooled

4 oz/115 g white chocolate,
   melted and cooled

sugar crystals

method

1 Place the eggs and sugar in a small heatproof bowl and set over a pan of gently simmering water. Whisk until thick and foamy. Remove the bowl from the pan and continue to whisk for 2 minutes.

2 Sift the flour, cocoa, cinnamon, cardamom, cloves, and nutmeg over the egg mixture, add the ground almonds and chopped peel and stir. Drop heaped teaspoonfuls of the cookie batter onto several cookie sheets lined with parchment paper, spreading them gently into smooth mounds and allowing room for expansion during cooking.

3 Bake in a preheated oven, 325°F/160°C, for 15–20 minutes, or until light brown and slightly soft to the touch. Let cool on the cookie sheets for 10 minutes, then transfer to wire racks to cool completely. Dip half the cookies in the melted semisweet chocolate and half in the white chocolate. Sprinkle with sugar crystals, let set, then serve.

checkerboard cookies

ingredients

MAKES 18

6 oz/175 g/3/4 cup butter, softened

6 tbsp confectioners' sugar

1 teaspoon vanilla extract or grated rind of 1/2 orange

9 oz/250 g/21/4 cups all-purpose flour

1 oz/25 g semisweet chocolate

a little beaten egg white

method

1 Beat the butter and confectioners' sugar in a mixing bowl until light and fluffy. Beat in the vanilla extract or grated orange rind. Gradually beat in the flour to form a soft dough. Use your fingers to incorporate the last of the flour and bring the dough together.

2 Melt the chocolate. Divide the dough in half and beat the melted chocolate into one half. Keeping each half of the dough separate, cover, and let chill for 30 minutes.

3 Roll out each piece of dough to a rectangle measuring 3 x 8 inches/7.5 x 20 cm and 3-cm/11/2-inches thick. Brush one piece of dough with a little egg white and place the other on top. Cut the block of dough in half lengthwise and turn over one half. Brush the side of one strip with egg white and butt the other up to it, so that it resembles a checkerboard.

4 Cut the block into thin slices and place each slice flat on a lightly greased cookie sheet, allowing enough room for the slices to spread out a little during cooking.

5 Bake in a preheated oven, 350°F/180°C, for about 10 minutes, until just firm. Let cool on the cookie sheets for a few minutes, before carefully transferring to a wire rack with a spatula. Let cool completely.

chocolate wheat cookies

ingredients

MAKES 20

6 tbsp butter, plus extra for
     greasing
$3^1/_2$ oz/100 g/$^1/_2$ cup raw
     demerara sugar
1 egg
1 oz/25 g/$^1/_4$ cup wheat germ
$4^1/_2$ oz/125 g/scant 1 cup
     whole-wheat flour
6 tbsp self rising flour, sifted
$4^1/_2$ oz/125 g chocolate

method

1 Beat the butter and sugar until fluffy.
Add the egg and beat well. Stir in the wheat
germ and flours. Bring the batter together with
your hands.

2 Roll rounded teaspoons of the batter into
balls and place on a greased cookie sheet,
allowing room for expansion during cooking.

3 Flatten the cookies slightly with a fork, then
bake in a preheated oven, 350°F/180°C, for
15–20 minutes, or until golden. Let cool on
the cookie sheet for a few minutes before
transferring to a wire rack to cool completely.

4 Melt the chocolate, then dip each cookie in
the chocolate to cover the bases and come a
little way up the sides. Let the excess
chocolate drip back into the bowl. Place the
cookies on a sheet of parchment paper and
let set in a cool place before serving.

hazelnut bites

ingredients

MAKES 24 COOKIES

4 oz/115 g/^{1}/$_2$ cup butter, plus
    extra for greasing
5 oz/140 g/^{3}/$_4$ cup raw
    brown sugar
1 egg
1 tbsp almond extract
5 oz/150 g/1 cup
    all-purpose flour
^{3}/$_4$ tsp baking powder
pinch of salt
7 oz/200 g/2 cups rolled oats
3 oz/85 g/^{1}/$_2$ cup semisweet
    chocolate chips
1^3/$_4$ oz/50 g/^{2}/$_3$ cup
    hazelnuts, toasted
    and chopped
7 oz/200 g semisweet
    chocolate, chopped into
    small pieces

method

1 Cream the butter and sugar together in a bowl. Add the egg and almond extract and beat well. In a separate bowl, sift together the flour, baking powder, and salt. Beat in the egg mixture. Stir in the oats, chocolate chips, and half of the hazelnuts.

2 Put 24 rounded tablespoonfuls of the dough onto a large, greased cookie sheet and flatten with a rolling pin. Transfer to a preheated oven, 350°F/180°C, and bake for 10 minutes, or until the cookies are golden brown.

3 Remove the cookies from the oven, then transfer to a wire rack and let them cool thoroughly. Put the chocolate pieces in a heatproof bowl over a pan of simmering water and heat until melted. Cover the tops of the cookies with melted chocolate, then top with a sprinkling of the remaining hazelnuts. Let cool on waxed paper. Store in an airtight container in the refrigerator before serving.

chocolate chip shortbread

ingredients

SERVES 8

4 oz/115 g butter, diced, plus
    extra for greasing

4 oz/115 g/generous $^3/_4$ cup
    all-purpose flour

2 oz/55 g/$^3/_8$ cup cornstarch

2oz/55 g/generous $^1/_4$ cup
    golden superfine sugar

1$^1/_2$ oz/40 g/$^1/_4$ cup
    semisweet chocolate chips

method

1 Sift the flour and cornstarch into a large mixing bowl. Stir in the sugar, then add the butter and rub it in until the mixture starts to bind together.

2 Turn into a greased 9-inch/23-cm loose-bottom fluted tart pan and press evenly over the base. Prick the surface with a fork. Sprinkle with the chocolate chips and press lightly into the surface.

3 Bake the shortbread in a preheated oven, 325°F/160°C, for 35–40 minutes, or until cooked but not browned. Mark into 8 portions with a sharp knife. Let cool in the pan for 10 minutes, then transfer to a wire rack to cool completely.

chocolate shortbread

ingredients

SERVES 4

7 oz/200 g butter, diced,
   plus extra for greasing

12 oz/350 g/2^2/$_3$ cups all-
   purpose flour, plus extra
   for dusting

2 tbsp unsweetened cocoa
   powder

5 oz/140 g/^{3}/$_4$ cup superfine
   sugar, plus extra for
   decorating

1 tbsp milk (optional)

method

1 Sift the flour and cocoa powder into a large bowl. Rub in the butter using your fingertips until the mixture resembles fine bread crumbs. Stir in the sugar. Using your hands, shape the mixture into a firm dough. If necessary, add a little milk.

2 Roll out the dough on a lightly floured work surface to a thickness of about ^{1}/$_2$ inch/1 cm. Stamp out fancy shapes using assorted cookie cutters about 2 inches/5 cm in diameter and 1 inch/2.5 cm deep. Alternatively, use a sharp knife to cut the dough into bars or fingers. Arrange the dough shapes on a large, greased cookie sheet, leaving enough space between them to allow them to spread during cooking.

3 Bake in a preheated oven, 350°F/180°C, for 30 minutes, or until golden. Remove from the oven, transfer to a wire rack, dust with superfine sugar, and let cool completely. Arrange on a serving plate and serve.

caramel chocolate shortbread

ingredients

MAKES 24

4 oz/115 g butter, plus extra
   for greasing
6 oz/175 g/^{3}/$_4$ cup plain flour
2 oz/55 g/^{1}/$_3$ cup golden
   superfine sugar

filling and topping

6 oz/175 g butter
4 oz/115 g/^{2}/$_3$ cup golden
   superfine sugar
3 tbsp corn syrup
14 oz/400 g canned
   condensed milk
7 oz/200 g plain chocolate,
   broken into pieces

method

1 Place the butter, flour and sugar in a food processor and process until it begins to bind together. Press the mixture into a greased and base-lined 23-cm/9-inch shallow square cake tin and smooth the top. Bake in a preheated oven, 350°F/180°C, for 20–25 minutes, or until golden.

2 Meanwhile, make the filling. Place the butter, sugar, syrup and condensed milk in a saucepan and heat gently until the sugar has melted. Bring to the boil and simmer for 6–8 minutes, stirring constantly, until the mixture becomes very thick. Pour over the shortbread base and leave to chill in the refrigerator until firm.

3 To make the topping, melt the chocolate and leave to cool, then spread over the caramel. Chill in the refrigerator until set. Cut the shortbread into 12 pieces with a sharp knife and serve.

cappuccino squares

ingredients

MAKES 15

8 oz/225 g butter, softened,
  plus extra for greasing
8 oz/225 g/generous
  1 1/2 cups self-rising flour
1 tsp baking powder
1 tsp unsweetened cocoa,
  plus extra for dusting
8 oz/225 g/generous 1 cup
  golden superfine sugar
4 eggs, beaten
3 tbsp instant coffee powder,
  dissolved in 2 tbsp hot water

white chocolate frosting

4 oz/115 g white chocolate,
  broken into pieces
2 oz/55 g butter, softened
3 tbsp milk
6 oz/175 g/1 3/4 cups
  confectioners' sugar

method

1 Sift the flour, baking powder, and cocoa into a bowl and add the butter, superfine sugar, eggs, and coffee. Beat well, by hand or with an electric whisk, until smooth, then spoon into a greased and base-lined shallow 11 x 7-inch/ 28 x 18-cm pan and smooth the top.

2 Bake in a preheated oven, 350°F/180°C, for 35–40 minutes, or until risen and firm, then turn out onto a wire rack and peel off the lining paper. Let cool completely. To make the frosting, place the chocolate, butter, and milk in a bowl set over a pan of simmering water and stir until the chocolate has melted.

3 Remove the bowl from the pan and sift in the confectioners' sugar. Beat until smooth, then spread over the cake. Dust the top of the cake with sifted cocoa, then cut into squares.

chocolate fudge brownies

ingredients

SERVES 16

7 oz/200 g lowfat soft cheese

$^1/_2$ tsp vanilla extract

9 oz/250 g/generous 1 cup
   superfine sugar

2 eggs

3$^1/_2$ oz/100 g/generous
   $^1/_3$ cup butter

3 tbsp unsweetened cocoa

3$^1/_2$ oz/100 g/$^3/_4$ cup self-
   rising flour, sifted

1$^3/_4$ oz/50 g/$^1/_3$ cup chopped
   pecans

fudge frosting

4 tbsp butter

1 tbsp milk

3$^1/_2$ oz/100 g/$^2/_3$ cup icing
   confectioners' sugar

2 tbsp unsweetened cocoa

pecans, to decorate (optional)

method

1 Beat together the cheese, vanilla extract, and 5 teaspoons of superfine sugar, then set aside.

2 Beat the eggs and remaining superfine sugar together until light and fluffy. Place the butter and cocoa in a small pan and heat gently, stirring until the butter melts and the mixture combines, then stir it into the egg mixture. Fold in the flour and nuts.

3 Pour half of the brownie mixture into a lightly greased 8-inch/20-cm square shallow cake pan and smooth the top. Carefully spread the soft cheese over it, then cover it with the remaining brownie mixture. Bake in a preheated oven, 350°F/180°C, for 40–45 minutes. Cool in the pan.

4 To make the frosting, melt the butter in the milk. Stir in the sugar and cocoa. Using a spatula, spread the frosting over the brownies and decorate with pecans (if using). Let the frosting set, then cut into squares to serve.

mocha brownies

ingredients

MAKES 16

2 oz/55 g butter, plus extra
   for greasing
4 oz/115 g semisweet
   chocolate, broken into
   pieces
6 oz/175 g/scant 1 cup
   brown sugar
2 eggs
1 tbsp instant coffee powder
   dissolved in 1 tbsp hot
   water, cooled
3 oz/85 g/scant $^2/_3$ cup
   all-purpose flour
$^1/_2$ tsp baking powder
2 oz/55 g/$^1/_3$ cup coarsely
   chopped pecans

method

1 Place the chocolate and butter in a heavy-bottom pan over low heat until melted. Stir and let cool.

2 Place the sugar and eggs in a large bowl and cream together until light and fluffy. Fold in the chocolate mixture and cooled coffee and mix thoroughly. Sift in the flour and baking powder and lightly fold into the mixture, then carefully fold in the pecans.

3 Pour the batter into a greased and base-lined 8-inch/20-cm square cake pan and bake in a preheated oven, 350°F/180°C, for 25–30 minutes, or until firm and a skewer inserted into the center comes out clean.

4 Let cool in the pan for a few minutes, then run a knife round the edge of the cake to loosen it. Turn the cake out onto a wire rack and peel off the lining paper. Let cool completely. When cold, cut into squares.

refrigerator cake

ingredients

MAKES 12 PIECES

2 oz/55 g/^{1}/$_3$ cup raisins

2 tbsp brandy

4 oz/115 g semisweet
   chocolate, broken
   into pieces

4 oz/115 g milk chocolate,
   broken into pieces

2 oz/55 g butter, plus extra
   for greasing

2 tbsp corn syrup

6 oz/175 g graham crackers,
   coarsely broken

2oz/55 g/^{1}/$_2$ cup slivered
   almonds, lightly toasted

1 oz/25 g/^{1}/$_8$ cup candied
   cherries, chopped

topping

3^1/$_2$ oz/100 g semisweet
   chocolate, broken
   into pieces

^{3}/$_4$ oz/20 g butter

method

1 Place the raisins and brandy in a bowl and let soak for 30 minutes. Put the chocolate, butter, and syrup in a pan and heat gently until melted.

2 Stir in the graham crackers, almonds, cherries, raisins, and brandy. Turn into a greased and base-lined 7-inch/18-cm shallow square pan and let cool. Cover and let chill in the refrigerator for 1 hour.

3 To make the topping, place the chocolate and butter in a small heatproof bowl and melt over a pan of gently simmering water. Stir and pour the chocolate mixture over the cookie base. Let chill in the refrigerator for 8 hours, or overnight. Cut into bars or squares to serve.

chocolates &
petits fours

This is where you really stray into chocolate paradise with some fabulous recipes. If you've ever gazed into the window of a chocolate shop and sighed wistfully, wishing you could try one of everything, here is your chance! Light, fluffy truffles, sophisticated chocolate liqueurs, rich, buttery fudge, wafer-thin florentines, and the aptly named rocky road bites—hidden lumps and bumps of marshmallows, walnuts, and apricots—they are all here for you to make. Some you will want to share with your family and friends, and some you might want to save for yourself!

Chocolates and petits fours are a great way to round off a special occasion meal, especially those that have a little liqueur added. Irish cream truffles, Italian chocolate truffles, rum truffles, chocolate orange collettes, chocolate liqueurs, and rum and chocolate cups will all go down well with after-dinner coffee. For family parties and festive occasions, try the fudge recipes, brazil nut brittle, nutty chocolate clusters, and of course those rocky road bites. For a really special, thoughtful gift, the chocolate mascarpone cups, mini chocolate cones, ladies' kisses, mini florentines, and chocolate biscotti look particularly attractive packaged in a pretty box.

And as a treat for yourself? Well, that's up to you!

white chocolate & pistachio truffles

ingredients

MAKES 26–30

3¹/₂ oz/100 g white chocolate, broken into pieces

¹/₂ oz/15 g butter

2¹/₂ fl oz/75 ml/generous ¹/₄ cup heavy cream

1 oz/25 g/¹/₈ cup shelled unsalted pistachios, finely chopped

confectioners' sugar, for coating

method

1 Place the chocolate, butter, and cream in a heatproof bowl and set over a pan of gently simmering water until melted, without stirring. Remove the bowl from the heat and stir gently, then stir in the nuts. Let cool, then cover with plastic wrap and let chill in the refrigerator for 8 hours, or overnight.

2 Line a cookie sheet with nonstick parchment paper. Take teaspoonfuls of the mixture and roll into balls. Place the truffles on the prepared cookie sheet and let chill for 2 hours, or until firm.

3 Just before serving, roll the truffles in confectioners' sugar to coat.

white chocolate truffles

ingredients

MAKES 12

2 tbsp unsalted butter

5 tbsp heavy cream

8 oz/225 g good-quality Swiss
  white chocolate

1 tbsp orange-flavored
  liqueur, optional

to finish

3¹/₂ oz/100 g white chocolate

method

1 Line a jelly roll pan with a sheet of baking parchment.

2 Place the butter and cream in a small pan and bring slowly to a boil, stirring constantly. Boil the mixture for 1 minute, then remove the pan from the heat.

3 Break the chocolate into pieces and add to the cream. Stir until melted, then beat in the orange-flavored liqueur (if using). Pour into the prepared pan and chill for about 2 hours, until firm.

4 Break off pieces of the truffle mixture and roll them into balls. Chill for an additional 30 minutes before finishing the truffles.

5 To finish, melt the white chocolate in a bowl set over a pan of gently simmering water. Dip the balls in the chocolate, allowing the excess to drip back into the bowl. Place on nonstick baking parchment, swirl the chocolate with the tines of a fork, and let harden.

irish cream truffles

ingredients

MAKES ABOUT 24

5 fl oz/150 ml/^{2}/$_3$ cup
    heavy cream
8 oz/225 g semisweet
    chocolate, broken
    into pieces
1 oz/25 g butter
3 tbsp Irish cream liqueur
4 oz/115 g white chocolate,
    broken into pieces
4 oz/115 g semisweet
    chocolate, broken into
    pieces

method

1 Heat the cream in a pan over low heat but do not let it boil. Remove from the heat and stir in the chocolate and butter. Let stand for 2 minutes, then stir until smooth. Stir in the liqueur. Pour the mixture into a bowl and let cool. Cover and let chill in the refrigerator for 8 hours, or overnight, until firm.

2 Line a cookie sheet with nonstick parchment paper. Take teaspoonfuls of the chilled chocolate mixture and roll into small balls. Place the balls on the prepared cookie sheet and let chill in the refrigerator for 2–4 hours, or until firm. Melt the white chocolate pieces and let cool slightly.

3 Coat half the truffles by spearing on thin skewers or toothpicks and dipping into the white chocolate. Transfer to a sheet of nonstick parchment paper to set. Melt the semisweet chocolate and let cool slightly, then use to coat the remaining truffles in the same way. Store the truffles in the refrigerator in an airtight container, separated by layers of waxed paper, for up to 1 week.

italian chocolate truffles

ingredients

MAKES 24

6 oz/175 g semisweet
  chocolate
2 tbsp Amaretto liqueur or
  orange-flavored liqueur
3 tbsp unsalted butter
4 tbsp confectioners' sugar
$1^3/_4$ oz/50 g/$^1/_2$ cup ground
  almonds
$1^3/_4$ oz/50 g grated chocolate

method

1 Melt the semisweet chocolate with the liqueur in a bowl set over a pan of hot water, stirring until well combined.

2 Add the butter and stir until it has melted. Stir in the confectioners' sugar and the ground almonds. Let the mixture stand in a cool place until it is firm enough to roll into 24 balls.

3 Place the grated chocolate on a plate and roll the truffles in the chocolate to coat them. Place the truffles in paper candy cases and let chill.

rum truffles

ingredients

MAKES 12

5^1/$_2$ oz/125 g semisweet
  chocolate

small piece of butter

2 tbsp rum

1^3/$_4$ oz/50 g/^{1}/$_2$ cup shredded
  coconut

3^1/$_2$ oz/100 g cake crumbs

6 tbsp confectioners' sugar

2 tbsp unsweetened cocoa

method

1 Break the chocolate into pieces and place in a bowl with the butter. Set the bowl over a pan of gently simmering water and stir until melted and combined.

2 Remove from the heat and beat in the rum. Stir in the shredded coconut, cake crumbs, and two-thirds of the confectioners' sugar. Beat until combined. Add a little extra rum if the mixture is stiff.

3 Roll the mixture into small balls and place them on a sheet of baking parchment. Chill until firm.

4 Strain the remaining confectioners' sugar onto a large plate. Strain the cocoa onto another plate. Roll half of the truffles in the confectioners' sugar until thoroughly coated and roll the remaining rum truffles in the cocoa.

5 Place the truffles in paper candy cases and let chill in the refrigerator.

chocolate orange collettes

ingredients

MAKES 20

10 oz/280 g semisweet
   chocolate, broken
   into pieces
$1/2$ tsp corn oil
5 fl oz/150 ml/$2/3$ cup
   heavy cream
finely grated rind of $1/2$ orange
1 tbsp Cointreau

to decorate

chopped nuts
fine strips of orange rind

method

1 Melt $5^{1}/_{2}$ oz/150 g of the chocolate with the oil and stir until mixed. Spread evenly over the inside of 20 double petit four cases, taking care to keep a good thickness round the edge. Let chill for 1 hour, or until set, then apply a second coat of chocolate, remelting if necessary. Let chill for 1 hour, or until completely set.

2 Place the cream and grated orange rind in a pan and heat until almost boiling. Remove from the heat, add the remaining chocolate pieces and stir until smooth. Return to the heat and stir until the mixture starts to bubble. Remove from the heat and stir in the Cointreau. Let cool, then peel the paper cases off the chocolate cups.

3 Beat the chocolate cream until thick, then spoon into a large pastry bag fitted with a fluted tip. Pipe the chocolate cream into the chocolate cases. Decorate some of the chocolate collettes with chopped nuts and some with a few strips of orange rind. Cover and keep in the refrigerator. Use within 2–3 days.

chocolate liqueurs

ingredients

MAKES 40

3^1/$_2$ oz/100 g semisweet
    chocolate

5 candied cherries, halved

10 hazelnuts or
    macadamia nuts

5fl oz/150ml/^{2}/$_3$ cup
    heavy cream

2 tbsp confectioners' sugar

4 tbsp liqueur

to finish

1^3/$_4$ oz/50 g semisweet
    chocolate, melted

a little white chocolate,
    melted, or white chocolate
    curls, or extra nuts and
    cherries

method

1 Line a cookie sheet with a sheet of baking parchment. Break the semisweet chocolate into pieces, place in a bowl and set over a pan of hot water. Stir until melted. Spoon the chocolate into 20 paper candy cases, spreading up the sides with a small spoon or brush. Place upside down on the cookie sheet and let set.

2 Carefully peel away the paper cases. Place a cherry or nut in the bottom of each cup.

3 To make the filling, place the heavy cream in a mixing bowl and sift the confectioners' sugar on top. Whisk the cream until it is just holding its shape, then whisk in the liqueur to flavor it.

4 Place the cream in a pastry bag fitted with a ^{1}/$_2$-inch/1-cm plain tip and pipe a little into each chocolate case. Let chill for 20 minutes.

5 To finish, spoon the semisweet chocolate over the cream to cover it and pipe the melted white chocolate on top, swirling it into the semisweet chocolate with a toothpick. Let harden. Alternatively, cover the cream with the melted semisweet chocolate and decorate with white chocolate curls before setting. If you prefer, place a small piece of nut or cherry on top of the cream, then cover with semisweet chocolate.

chocolate marzipans

ingredients

MAKES 30

1 lb/450 g marzipan

1 oz/25 g/generous ⅛ cup
candied cherries,
very finely chopped

confectioners' sugar,
for dusting

1 oz/25 g/generous ⅛ cup
preserved ginger, very
finely chopped

1¾ oz/50 g/generous ¼ cup
no-soak dried apricots,
very finely chopped

12 oz/350 g semisweet
chocolate, broken
into pieces

1 oz/25 g white chocolate

method

1 Line a cookie sheet with nonstick parchment paper. Divide the marzipan into 3 balls and knead each ball to soften it.

2 Work the candied cherries into 1 portion of the marzipan by kneading on a counter lightly dusted with confectioners' sugar. Do the same with the preserved ginger and another portion of marzipan, then the apricots and the third portion of marzipan. Form each flavored portion of marzipan into small balls, keeping the flavors separate.

3 Place the semisweet chocolate in a heatproof bowl and set over a pan of hot water. Stir until the chocolate has melted. Dip one of each flavored ball of marzipan into the melted chocolate by spiking each one with a toothpick, allowing the excess chocolate to drip back into the bowl.

4 Place the balls in clusters of the 3 flavors on the cookie sheet. Repeat with the remaining balls. Let chill in the refrigerator for 1 hour, or until set. Place the white chocolate in a small heatproof bowl and set over a pan of simmering water. Stir until the chocolate has melted. Drizzle a little over the tops of each cluster of marzipan balls. Let chill in the refrigerator for 1 hour, or until hard. Remove from the parchment paper, arrange on a plate and serve.

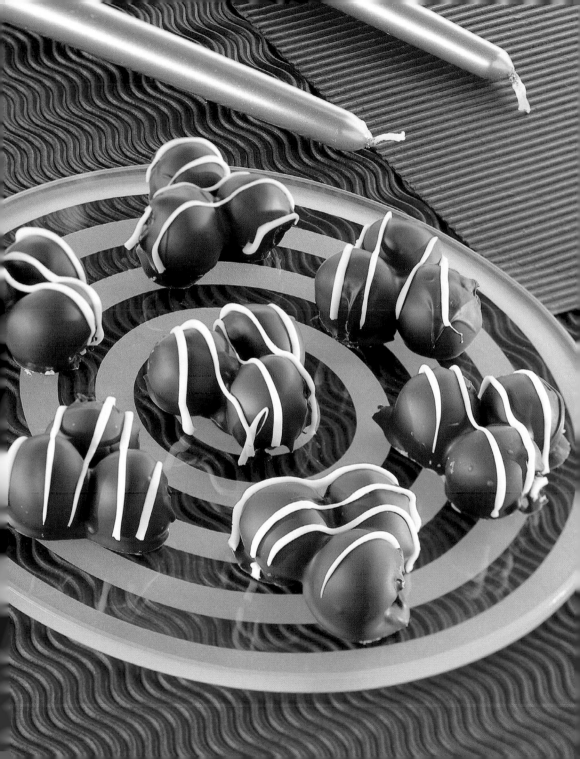

chocolate mascarpone cups

ingredients

MAKES 20

3 1/2 oz/100 g semisweet
   chocolate

filling

3 1/2 oz/100 g light or
   semisweet chocolate

1/4 tsp vanilla extract

7 oz/200 g mascarpone
   cheese

unsweetened cocoa, for dusting

method

1 Line a cookie sheet with a sheet of baking parchment. Break the semisweet chocolate into pieces, place in a bowl and set over a pan of hot water. Stir until melted. Spoon the chocolate into 20 paper candy cases, spreading up the sides with a small spoon or brush. Place the chocolate cups upside down on the cookie sheet and let set. When set, carefully peel away the paper cases.

2 To make the filling, melt the chocolate. Place the mascarpone cheese in a bowl and beat in the vanilla extract and melted chocolate until well combined. Let the mixture chill in the refrigerator, beating occasionally until firm enough to pipe.

3 Place the mascarpone filling in a pastry bag fitted with a star tip and pipe the mixture into the cups. Decorate with a dusting of cocoa.

mini chocolate cones

ingredients

MAKES 10

2³/₄ oz/75 g semisweet
chocolate

3¹/₂ fl oz/100 ml/generous
¹/₃ cup heavy cream

1 tbsp confectioners' sugar

1 tbsp crème de menthe

chocolate-covered coffee
beans,

to decorate (optional)

method

1 Cut 10 x 3-inch/7.5-cm circles of parchment paper. Shape each circle into a cone shape and secure with a piece of sticky tape.

2 Break the chocolate into pieces, place in a heatproof bowl, and set over a pan of hot water. Stir until the chocolate has melted. Using a small pastry brush or clean artist's brush, brush the inside of each cone with the melted chocolate.

3 Brush a second layer of chocolate on the inside of the cones and let chill in the refrigerator for 2 hours, or until set. Carefully peel away the paper.

4 Place the cream, confectioners' sugar and crème de menthe in a large bowl and whip until just holding its shape. Place in a pastry bag fitted with a star tip and pipe the mixture into the chocolate cones. Decorate the cones with chocolate-covered coffee beans, if using, and let chill in the refrigerator for 1–2 hours.

rum & chocolate cups

ingredients

SERVES 12

2 oz/55 g semisweet
  chocolate, broken
  into pieces
12 toasted hazelnuts

filling

4 oz/115 g semisweet
  chocolate, broken
  into pieces
1 tbsp dark rum
4 tbsp mascarpone cheese

method

1 To make the chocolate cups, place the semisweet chocolate in the top of a double boiler or in a heatproof bowl set over a pan of barely simmering water. Stir over low heat until the chocolate is just melted but not too runny, then remove from the heat. Spoon $1/2$ teaspoon of melted chocolate into a foil confectionery case and brush it over the base and up the sides. Coat 11 more foil cases in the same way and let set for 30 minutes. Let chill in the refrigerator for 15 minutes. If necessary, reheat the chocolate in the double boiler or heatproof bowl to melt it again, then coat the foil cases with a second, slightly thinner coating. Chill in the refrigerator for an additional 30 minutes.

2 To make the filling, place the chocolate in the top of a double boiler or in a heatproof bowl set over a pan of barely simmering water. Stir over low heat until melted and smooth, then remove from the heat. Let cool slightly, stir in the rum, and beat in the mascarpone cheese until smooth. Let cool completely, stirring occasionally.

3 Spoon the filling into a pastry bag fitted with a $1/2$-inch/1-cm star tip. Carefully peel away the confectionery cases from the chocolate cups. Pipe the filling into the cups and top each one with a toasted hazelnut.

easy chocolate fudge

ingredients

MAKES 25 PIECES

2³/₄ oz/75 g unsalted butter,
   cut into even-size pieces,
   plus extra for greasing
1 lb 2 oz/500 g semisweet
   chocolate
14 oz/400 g canned sweetened
   condensed milk
¹/₂ tsp vanilla extract

method

1 Lightly grease an 8-inch/20-cm square cake pan with butter. Break the chocolate into small pieces and place in a large, heavy-bottom pan with the butter and condensed milk.

2 Heat gently, stirring constantly, until the chocolate and butter melt and the mixture is smooth. Do not let boil. Remove from the heat. Beat in the vanilla extract, then beat the mixture for a few minutes until thickened. Pour it into the pan and level the top.

3 Let the mixture chill in the refrigerator for 1 hour, or until firm. Tip the fudge out onto a cutting board and cut into squares to serve.

pecan mocha fudge

ingredients

MAKES 80 PIECES

10 fl oz/300 ml/1¼ cups milk

2 lb 4 oz/1 kg golden
    granulated sugar

9 oz/250 g butter, plus extra
    for greasing

2 tbsp instant coffee granules

2 tbsp unsweetened cocoa

2 tbsp corn syrup

14 oz/400 g canned
    condensed milk

4 oz/115 g/½ cup shelled
    pecans, chopped

method

1 Grease a 12 x 9-inch/30 x 23-cm jelly roll pan. Place the milk, sugar, and butter in a large pan. Stir over gentle heat until the sugar has dissolved. Stir in the coffee granules, cocoa, syrup, and condensed milk.

2 Bring to a boil and boil steadily, whisking constantly, for 10 minutes, or until a temperature of 241°F/116°C has been reached on a sugar thermometer, or a small amount of the mixture forms a soft ball when dropped into cold water.

3 Let cool for 5 minutes, then beat vigorously with a wooden spoon until the mixture starts to thicken. Stir in the nuts. Continue beating until the mixture takes on a fudge-like consistency. Quickly pour into the prepared pan and let stand in a cool place to set. Cut the fudge into squares to serve.

rocky road bites

ingredients

MAKES 18

4^1/$_2$ oz/125 g light chocolate

2^1/$_2$ oz/50 g mini multi-colored marshmallows

1 oz/25 g/^{1}/$_4$ cup chopped walnuts

1 oz/25 g no-soak dried apricots, chopped

method

1 Line a cookie sheet with baking parchment and set aside.

2 Break the chocolate into small pieces and place in a large mixing bowl. Set the bowl over a pan of simmering water and stir until the chocolate has melted. Stir in the marshmallows, walnuts, and apricots, and toss in the melted chocolate until well covered.

3 Place heaping teaspoons of the mixture onto the prepared cookie sheet. Let chill in the refrigerator until set, then carefully remove from the baking parchment. Place in paper candy cases to serve, if wished.

brazil nut brittle

ingredients

MAKES 20

oil, for brushing

12 oz/350 g semisweet
chocolate, broken
into pieces

3 oz/85 g/scant ³/4 cup
shelled Brazil nuts,
chopped

6 oz/175 g white chocolate,
coarsely chopped

6 oz/175 g fudge, coarsely
chopped

method

1 Brush the bottom of an 8-inch/20-cm square cake pan with oil and line with parchment paper. Melt half the semisweet chocolate and spread in the prepared pan.

2 Sprinkle with the chopped Brazil nuts, white chocolate, and fudge. Melt the remaining semisweet chocolate pieces and pour over the top.

3 Let the brittle set, then break up into jagged pieces using the tip of a strong knife.

nutty chocolate clusters

ingredients

MAKES 30

6 oz/175 g white chocolate

3¹/₂ oz/100 g graham
    crackers

3¹/₂ oz/100 g/²/₃ cup
    chopped macadamia nuts
    or brazil nuts

1 oz/25 g preserved ginger,
    chopped (optional)

6 oz/175 g semisweet
    chocolate

method

1 Line a cookie sheet with a sheet of baking parchment. Break the white chocolate into small pieces and melt in a large mixing bowl set over a pan of gently simmering water.

2 Break the graham crackers into small pieces. Stir the crackers into the melted chocolate with the chopped nuts and preserved ginger (if using).

3 Place heaping teaspoons of the chocolate cluster mixture onto the prepared cookie sheet. Chill until set, then carefully remove from the baking parchment.

4 Melt the semisweet chocolate and let cool slightly. Dip the clusters into the chocolate, letting the excess drip back into the bowl. Return to the cookie sheet and let chill until set.

apricot & almond clusters

ingredients

MAKES 24–28

4 oz/115 g semisweet
  chocolate, broken
  into pieces

2 tbsp honey

4 oz/115g/²/₃ cup no-soak
  dried apricots, chopped

2 oz/55 g/³/₈ cup blanched
  almonds, chopped

method

1 Place the chocolate and honey in a bowl and set over a pan of gently simmering water until the chocolate has melted. Stir in the apricots and almonds.

2 Drop teaspoonfuls of the mixture into petit four cases. Let set for 2–4 hours, or until firm.

chocolate cherries

ingredients

MAKES 24

12 candied cherries

2 tbsp rum or brandy

9 oz/250 g marzipan

5 1/2 oz/125 g semisweet
    chocolate

extra light, semisweet,
    or white chocolate,
    to decorate (optional)

method

1 Line a cookie sheet with a sheet of baking parchment.

2 Cut the candied cherries in half and place in a small bowl. Add the rum or brandy and stir to coat. Let the cherries soak for at least 1 hour, stirring occasionally.

3 Divide the marzipan into 24 pieces and roll each piece into a ball. Press half a cherry into the top of each marzipan ball.

4 Break the chocolate into pieces, place in a bowl, and set over a pan of hot water. Stir until melted. Dip each candy into the melted chocolate using a toothpick, allowing the excess to drip back into the bowl. Place the coated cherries on the baking parchment and chill until set.

5 If wished, melt a little extra chocolate and drizzle it over the top of the coated cherries. Let set.

ladies' kisses

ingredients

MAKES 20

5 oz/140 g unsalted butter

4 oz/115 g/generous $1/2$ cup
    superfine sugar

1 egg yolk

4 oz/115 g/generous 1 cup
    ground almonds

6 oz/175 g/generous 1 cup
    all-purpose flour

2 oz/55 g semisweet
    chocolate, broken
    into pieces

2 tbsp confectioners' sugar

2 tbsp unsweetened cocoa

method

1 Beat the butter and sugar together in a bowl until pale and fluffy. Beat in the egg yolk, then beat in the almonds and flour. Continue beating until well mixed. Shape the dough into a ball, wrap in plastic wrap, and let chill in the refrigerator for $11/2$–2 hours.

2 Unwrap the dough, break off walnut-size pieces, and roll them into balls between the palms of your hands. Place the dough balls on 3 cookie sheets lined with parchment paper, allowing room for expansion during cooking. Bake in a preheated oven, 325°F/160°C, for 20–25 minutes, or until golden brown. Carefully transfer the cookies, still on the parchment paper, if using, to wire racks to cool.

3 Place the semisweet chocolate in a small heatproof bowl and set over a pan of barely simmering water, stirring constantly, until melted. Remove the bowl from the heat.

4 Remove the cookies from the parchment paper, if using, and spread the melted chocolate over the bases. Sandwich them together in pairs and return to the wire racks to cool. Dust with a mixture of confectioners' sugar and cocoa and serve.

mini florentines

ingredients

MAKES 40

3 oz/85 g/^{1}/$_3$ cup butter

2^3/$_4$ oz/75g/^{1}/$_3$ cup
superfine sugar

2 tbsp golden raisins or
raisins

2 tbsp chopped candied
cherries

2 tbsp chopped candied
ginger

1 oz/25 g sunflower seeds

3^1/$_2$ oz/100 g/^{3}/$_4$ cup
slivered almonds

2 tbsp heavy cream

6 oz/175 g semisweet
chocolate

method

1 Grease and flour 2 cookie sheets or line with baking parchment.

2 Gently heat the butter in a small pan until melted. Add the sugar, stir until dissolved, then bring the mixture to a boil. Remove from the heat and stir in the golden raisins or raisins, cherries, ginger, sunflower seeds, and almonds. Mix well, then beat in the cream.

3 Place small teaspoons of the fruit and nut mixture onto the prepared cookie sheet, allowing plenty of space for the mixture to spread. Bake in a preheated oven, at 350°F/180°C, for 10–12 minutes or until light golden in color.

4 Remove from the oven and, while still hot, use a circular cookie cutter to pull in the edges to form perfect circles. Let cool and go crisp before removing from the cookie sheet.

5 Break the chocolate into pieces, place in a bowl over a pan of hot water, and stir until melted. Spread most of the chocolate onto a sheet of baking parchment. When the chocolate is on the point of setting, carefully place the cookies flat-side down on the chocolate and let harden completely.

6 Cut around the florentines and remove from the baking parchment. Spread a little more chocolate on the coated side of the florentines and use a fork to mark waves in the chocolate. Let set and keep cool.

chocolate biscotti

ingredients

MAKES 16

1 egg

3½ oz/100 g/⅓ cup superfine sugar

1 tsp vanilla extract

4½ oz/125 g/1 cup all-purpose flour

½ tsp baking powder

1 tsp ground cinnamon

1¾ oz/50 g semisweet chocolate, chopped coarsely

1¾ oz/50 g/½ cup toasted slivered almonds

1¾ oz/50 g/⅓ cup pine nuts

method

1 Whisk the egg, sugar, and vanilla extract in a mixing bowl with an electric mixer until thick and pale—ribbons of mixture should trail from the whisk as you lift it.

2 Sift the flour, baking powder, and cinnamon into a separate bowl, then sift into the egg mixture and fold in gently. Stir in the coarsely chopped semisweet chocolate, toasted slivered almonds, and pine nuts.

3 Turn out onto a lightly floured counter and shape into a flat log, 9-inches/23-cm long and ¾-inch/1.5-cm wide. Transfer to a large, lightly greased cookie sheet.

4 Bake in a preheated oven, 350°F/180°C, for 20–25 minutes or until golden. Remove the cookie log from the oven and let cool for 5 minutes or until firm.

5 Transfer the log to a cutting board. Using a serrated bread knife, cut the log on the diagonal into slices about ½ inch/1 cm thick and arrange them on the cookie sheet. Cook for 10–15 minutes, turning halfway through the cooking time.

6 Let cool for about 5 minutes, then transfer to a wire rack to cool.